my revision notes

AQA GCSE (9–1)

RELIGIOUS STUDIES
SPECIFICATION B

Kevin O'Donnell
with Jan Hayes

HODDER
EDUCATION
AN HACHETTE UK COMPANY

Imprimatur: + Vincent Nichols (Archbishop of Westminster)

Nihil obstat: Terry Tastad (Censor)
Date: 7 December 2017

The *Nihil Obstat* and *Imprimatur* are a declaration that a book or pamphlet is considered to be free from doctrinal or moral error. It is not implied that those who have granted the *Nihil Obstat* or *Imprimatur* agree with the contents, opinion or statements expressed.

Acknowledgements

The Publishers would like to thank the following for permission to reproduce copyright material.

The Bible: Quotations from the Revised Standard Version Edition of the Bible: Revised Standard Version of the Bible, copyright © 1946, 1952, and 1971 the Division of Christian Education of the National Council of the Churches of Christ in the United States of America. Used by permission. All rights reserved.; **The Catechism of the Catholic Church**: Latin text copyright © Libreria Editrice Vaticana, Citta del Vaticano 1993

Every effort has been made to trace all copyright holders, but if any have been inadvertently overlooked, the Publishers will be pleased to make the necessary arrangements at the first opportunity.

Although every effort has been made to ensure that website addresses are correct at time of going to press, Hodder Education cannot be held responsible for the content of any website mentioned in this book. It is sometimes possible to find a relocated web page by typing in the address of the home page for a website in the URL window of your browser.

Hachette UK's policy is to use papers that are natural, renewable and recyclable products and made from wood grown in sustainable forests. The logging and manufacturing processes are expected to conform to the environmental regulations of the country of origin.

Orders: please contact Bookpoint Ltd, 130 Park Drive, Milton Park, Abingdon, Oxon OX14 4SE. Telephone: (44) 01235 827720. Fax: (44) 01235 400401. Email education@bookpoint.co.uk Lines are open from 9 a.m. to 5 p.m., Monday to Saturday, with a 24-hour message answering service. You can also order through our website: www.hoddereducation.co.uk.

ISBN: 9781 510 418 363

First published in 2018 by
Hodder Education,
An Hachette UK Company
Carmelite House
50 Victoria Embankment
London EC4Y 0DZ

www.hoddereducation.co.uk

Impression number   10   9   8   7   6   5   4   3   2   1

Year   2021   2020   2019   2018

Cover photo © Arthimedes/Shutterstock.com

Typeset in Bembo Std Regular 11/13 by Integra Software Services Pvt. Ltd., Pondicherry, India

Printed in Spain

A catalogue record for this title is available from the British Library.

Contents

Component 1: Catholic Christianity

1 Creation
- 8 Forms of expression – art
- 10 Beliefs and teachings
- 12 Sources of authority
- 14 Practices

2 Incarnation
- 16 Forms of expression – symbol and incarnation
- 18 Beliefs and teachings
- 20 Sources of authority
- 22 Practices

3 The triune god
- 24 Forms of expression – music and the glory of God
- 26 Beliefs and teachings
- 28 Sources of authority
- 30 Practices

4 Redemption
- 32 Forms of expression – architecture and design
- 34 Beliefs and teachings
- 36 Sources of authority
- 38 Practices – Eucharist and Redemption

5 Church and the Kingdom of God
- 40 Forms of expression – drama and the faith journey
- 42 Beliefs and teachings
- 44 Sources of authority
- 46 Practices – the Church as the body of Christ

6 Eschatology: Christian life, death and eternity
- 48 Forms of expression – artefact and eschatology
- 50 Beliefs and teachings
- 52 Sources of authority
- 54 Practices – liturgies of life and death

Component 2: Perspectives on faith

7 Judaism – beliefs and teachings
- 62 Key beliefs
- 67 The covenant and the mitzvot

REVISED TESTED EXAM READY

8 Judaism – practices

74 The synagogue and worship

79 Family life and festivals

8 Theme A: Religion, relationships and families

86 Relationships and the human condition – love and sexualiy: communion and complementarity

88 Perspectives on relationships – marriage, cohabitation, divorce and separation

90 Families and responsibilities – roles of men, women and children

92 Dialogue 4: Gender, equality and discrimination – equality between men and women

9 Theme B: Religion, peace and conflict

94 Christian perspectives on human violence, justice, forgiveness and reconciliation

96 Christian perspectives on social justice and just war

98 Holy war and pacifism

100 Christian perspectives on terrorism and Christian initiatives in conflict resolution and peace making

10 Theme C: Religion, human rights and social justice

102 Human rights and religious freedom

104 Perspectives on wealth

106 Perspectives on poverty

108 Prejudice and discrimination

11 Theme D: St Mark's Gospel – the life of Jesus

110 The early ministry of Jesus

112 The later ministry of Jesus

114 The final days in Jerusalem

116 Significance and importance

12 Theme E: St Mark's Gospel as a source of spiritual truth

118 The Kingdom of God

120 Jesus' relationships with those disregarded by society

122 Faith and discipleship

124 Significance and importance

133 **Now test yourself answers**

REVISED TESTED EXAM READY

Get the most from this book

These revision notes will help you to revise for AQA's GCSE (9–1) Religious Studies Specification B. Everyone has to decide his or her own revision strategy, but it is essential to review your work, learn it and test your understanding.

These revision notes will help you to do that in a planned way, topic by topic. This book aims to give you the essentials that should serve as a reminder of what you will have covered in your course and allow you to bring together your own learning and understanding.

It is essential to review your work, learn it and test your understanding. Tick each box in the contents page when you have:
- revised and understood a topic
- checked your understanding
- practised the exam questions

You can also keep track of your revision by ticking off each topic heading in the book. You may find it helpful to add your own notes as you work through each topic.

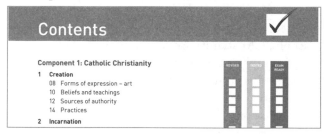

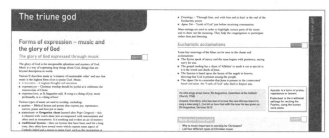

Features to help you succeed

Key terms

Clear, concise definitions of essential key terms are provided where they first appear. Key words from the specification are highlighted in bold throughout the book.

Key quotes

It is crucial that you can write about religious teachings in your exam. Almost all the questions demand this. This book includes many teachings to use, but you should look to add your own too.

Now test yourself

These short, knowledge-based questions provide the first step in testing your learning. Answers are at the back of the book.

Exam practice

Practice exam questions are provided for each topic, at the end of Component 1 and Component 2. Use them to consolidate your revision and practise your exam skills.

Online

Go online to find examiner-commentaries on sample Exam Practice questions, which will help you to assess your answers. You will find these at www.hoddereducation.co.uk/myrevisionnotes

How the assessment works

In your course you will have studied two components. Each component is examined in one written exam, 1 hour and 45 minutes in length.

Component 1

Catholic Christianity, covering Catholic beliefs, teachings, practices, sources of authority and forms of expression in relation to six topics:
- Creation
- Incarnation
- The Triune God
- Redemption
- Church
- Eschatology.

Whether you studied Route A or Route B, you will need to revise all of the content for Component 1, Catholic Christianity.

You will have one exam paper for Component 1. This paper will be worth 96 marks (plus 5 marks for SPaG), and will count for 50% of your GCSE.

The exam will be set on four of the six topics, and you must answer all questions that are set. Each topic will be examined by one five-part question, made up of questions worth of 1, 2, 4, 5 and 12 marks.

Component 2

One other religion: Islam OR Judaism *and* Contemporary ethical issues through religious and non-religious perspectives OR St Mark's Gospel.

If you have studied Route A, for Component 2 you will be required to answer questions on either Islam or Judaism, plus two ethical studies Themes (chosen from Themes A–C).
- Theme A: Religion, relationships and families
- Theme B: Religion, peace and conflict
- Theme C: Religion, human rights and social justice.

If you have studied Route B, for Component 2 you will be required to answer questions on either Islam or Judaism, plus both textual studies themes (Themes D–E).
- Theme D: St Mark's Gospel – the life of Jesus
- Theme E: St Mark's Gospel as a source of spiritual truth.

This Revision Guide covers all of this content apart from Islam. Do not use the material on the Chapters that you did not study in class.

You will have one exam paper for Component 2. This paper will be worth 96 marks (plus 5 marks for SPaG), and will count for 50% of your GCSE.

Section A (Judaism or Islam) There will be two five-part questions per religion, made up of questions worth of 1, 2, 4, 5 and 12 marks. You must answer both questions on the religion that you have studied.

Section B (Themes) There will be one five-part question per theme, made up of questions worth of 1, 2, 4, 5 and 12 marks. You must answer one question on each of two themes that you have studied.

Introduction to key issues in the specification

Diversity of religion in Britain

The specification asks for an awareness of Catholic Christianity and different faiths and non-religious beliefs in contemporary British society.

The main religious tradition of Britain is Christianity, which you have studied in depth. You need to also be aware that religious traditions in Great Britain are diverse, and include Buddhism, Hinduism, Islam, Judaism, Sikhism, and other religious and non-religious beliefs such as atheism and humanism. Although parts of the syllabus focus mainly on Catholic Christianity or Judaism as living faiths, mention should sometimes be made of the beliefs of others.

Diversity within Christianity

There can be diverse views within a faith. For example, with views of authority in the Church, Catholic and Protestant Christians will disagree: the Pope is the head of the Catholic Church but his authority is not recognised by Protestant churches. Another example would be attitude to homosexuality and though tolerance for all is taught by all Christian traditions as individuals, views differ on the morality of sexual relationships.

Foundations of Catholic Christianity

The Catholic faith is based upon three sources of authority: Scripture, Tradition and Magisterium.
- **Scripture** looks at the Old and New Testaments as a foundational set of texts, the New Testament originating from some of the Apostles and their followers, many of whom had been with Christ and knew his teaching. Scripture for Catholics conveys the Word of God.
- When the Church speaks of **Tradition** it means content that derives ultimately from Christ and the Apostles; material that was not explicitly in Scripture but is in accord with it. Thus the Church describes a single source of the Word of God, but two streams that convey it, Scripture and Tradition.
- **Magisterium** comes from the Latin 'Magister' or 'Teacher'. In the magisterium, the bishops, along with the Pope, guard Tradition and its development and application in modern times. They seek to keep faithful to what the Church has received from Christ and the first Christians, and to be respectful and faithful to what their forebears have stated.

Religious teachings

Key quotes are included throughout this Revision Guide. These come from Scripture, from the Catechism of the Catholic Church, and sometimes from other relevant sources, such as the writings of the saints.

The Catechism of the Catholic Church is a collection of sections covering all aspects of the Catholic faith. Abridged versions of this are available such as 'A Compendium of the Catechism of the Catholic Church' and 'YouCat', aimed at youth. The faith is set out in the Catechism in four sections:
- The Profession of Faith (looking at the Apostles Creed)
- The Celebration of the Christian Mystery (Liturgy and the sacraments)
- Life in Christ (covering morality and the Ten Commandments)
- Christian Prayer (including the Lord's Prayer)

Creation

Forms of expression – art

Michelangelo's *The Creation of Adam*

REVISED

The Creation of Adam is painted on the ceiling of the Sistine Chapel in Rome. It depicts God as an old man in the sky, carried by angels, reaching out and touching the finger of **Adam**, who rests upon solid ground. It reflects Catholic beliefs about God and **Creation** in the following ways:

- The Catholic belief that human beings are dependent upon God as their Creator for the gift of life; the divine touch brings Adam to life.
- Human beings are in the **image of God**, unlike other animals.
- The creation of all living things and the world is seen as good and important by the Creator; Adam is pictured as beautiful.
- God is high above Adam suggesting greater power, significance and mystery.
- There is a hint of mystery as God is surrounded by what appears to be a brain-shaped shroud. The artist was trying to show that we are limited in how we understand God because we tend to picture God in human terms.
- Picturing God as an old man suggests wisdom and age, i.e. **eternity**.

Controversial aspects

- Adam and God are pictured as the same size. This could give the impression that human beings are as important as God.
- God is a mystery and Spirit, invisible and with no physical form in Christian belief. God is omnipresent, everywhere at once, and not a single thing or shape. This is only a symbolic picture, and picturing God in human images is known as **anthropomorphism**.

Adam is the first human being. His name means 'of the earth'.

Creation is the origin of the universe coming to be from a designer and a spiritual force (i.e. God).

The **Image of God** is something about human beings that reflects the Creator, reason, morality, spirituality and creativity.

Eternity is life without end, no beginning and no ending.

Anthropomorphism is picturing or thinking about God in human form.

Other Christian art that expresses belief in Creation

Other examples of the creation of Adam and Eve are frequent in Christian art, such as stained-glass windows. An example is found in the Cathedral of St Michael and St Gudula in Brussels, Belgium. It was designed by Jean-Baptiste Capronnier and shows God as an old man, but this time slightly bigger than Adam and Eve. He raises his hand and one finger in blessing and creative power.

Modern paintings are more symbolic such as *From the heart of God has sprung all that exists* by Elizabeth Wang. This shows three interlinked persons, almost formless, surrounding the earth with sacred flames. This painting reflects Catholic beliefs about God and creation in a different way from Michelangelo's *The Creation of Adam*:

- The great size of God compared to the world reflects belief in the superiority and greatness of God over his creation.
- The descending hand symbolises God coming into the world in revelation, but being largely hidden. This reflects the Catholic belief that God is mysterious and beyond human understanding.
- The abstract, modern style of Elizabeth Wang reflects the sense of mystery and that God, as our creator, is beyond our understanding.

Now test yourself

TESTED

1 How does Michelangelo show that God is a mystery in his painting *The Creation of Adam*?
2 How does Michelangelo show that human beings have dignity and are more special than other living creatures?
3 *From the heart of God has sprung all that exists* by Elizabeth Wang has a very different way of exploring the idea of God as creator. How does it show this?
4 How is anthropomorphism shown in Michelangelo's *The Creation of Adam*, and how is this rejected in Elizabeth Wang's *From the heart of God has sprung all that exists*?

Beliefs and teachings

Creation and the nature of God in Genesis 1 and 2

There are two versions of the creation story in the opening chapters of the Bible. The first, Genesis 1, is a poem imagining the creation happening in seven stages or 'days' (often interpreted as 'periods of time'). This teaches that:

● God is the Creator, as all things and life come from him. They did not just happen by random chance and the world is formed by an intelligence and has order.
● God creates through his **Word**.
● God is **omnipotent** – God is the ultimate power behind everything.
● God is **transcendent** – God is beyond the physical universe and a mystery beyond our understanding.

Genesis 2 is more of a parable, using symbols and myths. Catholics see this as not literally true, but as spiritually true. Compare the famous story of 'The Tortoise and the Hare'; this is not literally true but is has a true message. Genesis 2 teaches:

● God is the Creator and takes time to create Adam as a special type of being, of the earth and yet different from other animals.
● God is the giver of all life and gives free will to human beings.

> The **Word** is God's power in action, spoken, expressed, communicated.
>
> **Omnipotent** means that God is beyond and behind all things, the ultimate power.
>
> **Transcendent** is that God is beyond human understanding and beyond the physical universe.

Human beings made in the image of God

In Genesis 1, human beings are made at the end of the stages of Creation. They are the pinnacle of creation.

● They are made in God's image and likeness.
● Being made in the image of God means they have reason, free will, a moral sense, a spiritual sense and are creative. It does not mean that humans literally look like God, in a physical sense; they are like God 'inside'.
● If every human being bears the image of God, all are equal and to be respected and valued regardless of race, age or situation. This is why Catholics support human rights.

> So God created man in his own image, in the image of God he created him; male and female he created them. (Genesis 1:27)

In Genesis 2, the first human is named Adam (meaning 'of the earth').

● Adam is made of the dust of the earth and receives the breath of life from God.
● Adam is greater than the animals who are made after him, and they are not on his level.
● Adam names the animals, showing his power to look after the world.
● Eve is created from Adam to be an equal companion after the animals are not sufficient. Men and women are made of the same material things and are equal in dignity.
● Adam and Eve are given free will.
● Adam and Eve were blessed with the Garden and the possibility of eating from the Tree of Life; God is benevolent.
● Adam and Eve are given the responsibility of looking after the earth.

The influence of this on Catholic views

The belief that humans are made in the image of God influences views about free will, **stewardship**, the dignity of human beings, and the **sanctity of life**:

- Free will is the ability to choose our actions and between right and wrong. No one should be forced to believe or do anything against their conscience.
- Stewardship means that human beings have been entrusted with the care of the earth, looking after it for God. They have been given power to subdue nature, but sadly, this can mean that they abuse it, too.
- As humans are made in the image of God, all human beings are created equal with the same rights; they all have dignity. Human relationships are important morally and spiritually, this is shown by God creating Eve for Adam.
- Sanctity of life means that each human life is special, unique and sacred because it is a gift from God. Catholics believe that life, from conception to death, should be valued and protected.

> **Stewardship** is the idea that humans have responsibility to look after the earth.
>
> The **sanctity of life** is that each human life is a gift from God and is sacred.

Every person, from the first moment of his life in the womb, has an inviolable dignity, because from all eternity God willed, loved, created and redeemed that person and destined him for eternal happiness. (*YouCat*, page 280)

Now test yourself

TESTED ☐

1 How does the account of creation in Genesis chapter 1 show that God is transcendent?
2 How does Genesis 2 show that human beings are special?
3 What responsibility is given to humanity in the creation stories?
4 What four points does the Catholic Church learn from the Genesis stories of creation?

Sources of authority

Origin and structure of the Bible

The Bible is a collection of books. The word 'bible' comes from the Greek *biblia* meaning 'the books'. These would have each been written on individual scrolls at first. The Bible came together over many years:

- oral – the stories, sayings and laws would have been passed on for many years through spoken words, poems and songs
- written – the stories were gradually written down. This would have been at least from 1,000 BCE onwards
- collected – the different scrolls were collected together by the early Church and the collection of books that make up the Bible was finally settled by Pope Damascus in 382 CE. This agreed content of the Bible recognised by the Catholic Church is known as the agreed '**canon**' or rule of contents.

The Bible contains different types of literature such as laws, stories, history, sayings, prayers, poems and songs of praise.

Apostles are the first followers of Jesus, either the original 12 disciples or others who joined them.

Biblia is Greek for 'books'. The Bible is a library of individual books written at different times with different types of literature.

Canon is a rule or list of the books that should be included in the Bible.

Inspiration is 'God breathed', divine influence on the Biblical authors.

Prophecy is speaking the word of God to the people of the time, or looking into the future.

The Old and New Testaments

There are two main parts to the Bible. The Old Testament is the story of the Jewish people and their hope of the Messiah to come. This is made up of:
- the Torah (Law) – the first five books
- History – stories of the people of Israel
- Wisdom – prayers, psalms of praise, wise sayings
- **Prophecy** – the words of inspired men (prophets) who brought messages from God.

The New Testament is based upon the life of Jesus, the **Apostles** and their teachings. The New Testament is made up of:
- the Gospels – the four Gospels of Matthew, Mark, Luke and John contain the 'good news' about Jesus. Seen as the most important of the books
- Acts of the Apostles – some stories of the early Church
- Epistles (letters) – written by Saints Paul, Peter and John
- Revelation – a symbolic book teaching about the end of time and the return of Christ.

These books were selected from other early Christian books because they were based upon the work of the Apostles or their disciples. They were all written before the end of the first century. They agreed with the main Christian teachings and were respected by all Christians. Other books were rejected.

Inspiration of the Bible as the revealed Word of God

The 'Word of God' refers to God's message; God acting in the world. The Bible did not fall from heaven nor was it discovered whole and complete. It was written down over more than a thousand years by many people.

Christians believe that the writers of the Bible were inspired by God. '**Inspire**' comes from the Latin word meaning 'breathe into'. According to Genesis, God breathed life into creation. They believe that God called, guided and inspired various people down the ages to say something important, including the Bible writers. They were inspired but used their own words to express this.

It was not magic; they were not in a trance writing automatically. They prayed and thought about what they wrote.

The Prophets, for example, spoke a message that was either for their day ('forthtelling') or for the future ('foretelling'). They mainly spoke for their day. The Word of God was seen to come to them in these two ways.

The Gospels say that Jesus is the Word made flesh, the fullest revelation of God possible to humanity in this world.

The Genesis creation accounts

The Bible contains many different types of writing. The stories of creation in Genesis 1 and 2 are an example. Scholars debate when the two stories were written down, many thinking that Genesis 1 came from about 400 BCE and Genesis 2 from about 900 BCE, though oral versions of these might have been around for a long time before.

Different Christian denominations interpret the Genesis stories in different ways. Catholics believe:

● that they are not to be read literally as historically or scientifically accurate accounts of creation
● that they are ideas about the origin of the world using poetry, symbols and mythology. They contain truths that are morally and spiritually true for all time. The Genesis stories are about beginnings and meanings. They tell why the world was made, and not how
● that they can therefore believe in both the Genesis creation accounts and scientific explanations of creation (evolution/the big bang).

However, **fundamentalist** Christians take the Genesis stories literally, arguing that scientists are wrong and that we have to take everything in the Bible at face value. Catholics believe that this is what is known as a '**category mistake**'.

> **Category mistake** is thinking that a writing is to be taken as one form and not another, history instead of poetry, for example.
>
> **Fundamentalist** is a believer who takes all the Bible literally, at face value.
>
> **Natural law** is following the order of nature as created, and how human beings are made. 'Avoiding evil and doing good.'

> Since God speaks in Sacred Scripture through men in human fashion, the interpreter of Sacred Scripture [...] should carefully investigate what meaning the sacred writers really intended and what God wanted to manifest by means of their words.

Natural law

Catholics believe that all of the universe was created by God and that everything God created was good. As humans were created by God, Catholics believe that we all have an inbuilt sense of what is morally right and wrong and they call this '**natural law**'. A basic rule is 'do good and avoid evil', and humans know what is good and evil and they can work this out with their own reason rather than having to be told.

Catholics believe in the 'sanctity of life' – that because all humans are made by God, in his image human life is sacred. Natural law says that because human life is sacred, it should be preserved. So Catholics would be against procedures such as abortion and euthanasia because they end life.

Science and religion

The Church has always been involved in scientific observations and theories. The friar Roger Bacon developed what we know as the scientific method of experiments and observation. The friar Gregor Mendel developed the idea of genetics. Friar George's Lemaitre first thought up the idea of the big bang.

However, lots of people view science and religion as incompatible. One of the documents produced by the Second Vatican Council (1962–65) was *Gaudium et Spes*, which looked at the relationship between the Catholic Church and the modern world, including its relationship with science.

Gaudium et Spes encouraged the link between science and faith, saying that scientific investigation done properly doesn't conflict with faith. It is a way of helping people understand more about what God created. However, it should be remembered that all of creation is dependent upon God.

Now test yourself

1 How was the Bible involved in oral, written and collected activities?
2 List the different types of writing found in the Bible.
3 What are the four sections of the New Testament?
4 What is meant by the sanctity of life?
5 Give two examples of how the Catholic Church sees no contradiction between science and faith.

TESTED

Practices

Care of the environment and love of your neighbour

The environment is part of God's creation, which is a gift of love. Human beings are asked to care for it. Everything is connected; we depend upon the earth and its resources to live. Not caring properly for the environment affects other people, particularly the poorest, as climate change affects crops and can cause drought, and pollution spoils water supplies.

'Love your neighbour as yourself' (Leviticus 19:18) was an Old Testament command. Jesus also taught that this is the greatest commandment in Mark 12:29–31; this is to love God and your neighbour. The parable of the Good Samaritan (Luke 10:25–37) also emphasises this, reminding people that everyone is our neighbour regardless of race or religion.

People are also asked to be neighbourly to the environment, respecting God's world and respecting others who rely upon it; everything is connected.

> Jesus answered, 'The first is, "Hear, O Israel: The Lord our God, the Lord is one; and you shall love the Lord your God with all your heart, and with all your soul, and with all your mind, and with all your strength." The second is this, "You shall love your neighbour as yourself." There is no other commandment greater than these.' (Mark 12:29–31)

Stewardship

As seen in the Genesis stories, humans are asked to be **stewards** of the earth, to look after its resources. They are empowered to do so as they are in the image of God, with free will, reason, morality and creativity.

Pope Francis said, 'A fragile world, entrusted by God to human care, challenges us to devise ways of directing, developing and limiting our power.' (*Laudato Si* 78). The Church, following the Bible, teaches that human beings have power over the earth and we need to use it responsibly, caring for the environment, for each other and using technology wisely and not greedily.

Catholics should be concerned to take action where they can:

Locally

- Save energy in the home.
- Use sustainable energy such as solar power.
- Use public transport or cycle sometimes.
- Recycle goods and reuse where possible.
- Avoid using things such as plastic bags where possible.
- Eat less meat for health reasons and to allow more investment in grains and vegetable production.

Nationally

- Write to MPs and the Prime Minister to encourage less pollution and more sustainable energy.
- Support products from environmentally friendly producers.
- Campaign to get companies to use more environmentally friendly procedures.

Globally

- Campaign for governments to implement agreements such as Rio+20 (the United Nations Conference on Sustainable Development).
- Support groups such as **CAFOD** and their environmental campaigns.
- Support wildlife charities and campaign against abuse.

CAFOD and sustainability

Sustainability means to care for the earth and not use up its natural resources. It means preserving the environment for others and future generations. Pope Francis teaches in *Laudato Si* 92–93 that justice and peace issues cannot be separated from care of the environment because environmental issues affect the poor and their way of life.

CAFOD (The Catholic Agency for Overseas Development) is a charity that seeks to work with the poor and to help the environment. They encourage better local farming methods, cleaner water supplies and cleaner, more efficient energy. For example, in Uganda, the villagers of Nakambi have been taught how to build wood-burning stoves that use fewer logs and that produce less smoke. The air is cleaner and fewer trees are cut down. They also sell these stoves at the local market to make an income.

This is a way of recognising the goodness of God's creation. It is not to be destroyed and wasted.

> **CAFOD** is the Catholic Agency for Overseas Development.
>
> **Stewardship** is to look after the earth.
>
> **Sustainability** is to work for sustainable energy and farming, to protect natural resources for future generations.

Now test yourself

TESTED

1 What does Leviticus 19:18 say?
2 What is the greatest commandment in Mark 12:29–31?
3 How does care of the environment link with care of neighbour?
4 What is sustainability?
5 What is meant by stewardship of the earth in Genesis?

Incarnation

Forms of expression – symbol and incarnation

Key Christian symbols

REVISED

Human beings often express thoughts and feelings in pictures or symbols. Christianity has a number of symbols to express belief in the **incarnation** (God becoming man in Jesus). These are some examples, and they are all **monograms** – images made up of letters.

- **ICTHUS** – this symbol forms the outline of a fish, and the word *icthus* means 'fish' in Greek. The letters come from the statement: 'Jesus Christ, Son of God, Saviour' (in Greek this is *Iesous Christos, Theou (H)uios, Soter*). This symbolises belief in the incarnation because Jesus Christ is both son of God (the divine second person of the Trinity) and saviour (God incarnate in a man who died on the cross.).
- **Alpha and omega** – these are the first and last letters of the Greek alphabet. Jesus called himself the 'Alpha and the Omega' in Revelation 1:8. This means that he was and is and will be forever. It symbolises Jesus' divinity – the fact that he is God.
- *Chi-Rho* – This is made up of the first two letters of 'Christ' in Greek. 'Christ' is a Greek translation of the Hebrew 'messiah' which means coming king and redeemer of the world. Old copies of the Gospels, such as the Lindisfarne Gospels, used this symbol alongside images of the birth of Jesus.

> **Alpha and omega** are the first and last letters of the Greek alphabet.
>
> *Chi-Rho* are the first two letters of 'Christ' in Greek.
>
> The **crucifix** is an image of Jesus on the cross.
>
> **Incarnation** is the belief that God became man in Jesus.
>
> **ICTHUS** is the fish sign that spells out 'Jesus Christ, Son of God, Saviour'.
>
> An **idol** is any object that is worshipped instead of God.
>
> A **monogram** is a symbol made up of letters.

The incarnation and Catholic views about art and imagery

REVISED

Christians in general have been largely happy with the use of religious images. This is not the case in some other religions, for example Judaism and Islam do not allow images of God in case the images are worshipped instead of God. Christians, sometimes, have followed this idea. The iconoclasts in the eighth and ninth centuries CE removed mosaics and icons of Christ and the saints, sometimes replacing these with an image of a simple cross. Christians at the time of the Reformation who followed Protestant views also rejected images, often destroying statues or whitewashing walls where paintings of Christ and the saints were depicted.

However, Catholics believe that because of the incarnation, religious art is acceptable. They believe that because the invisible, transcendent God made himself known and visible in human form in Jesus, then it is perfectly acceptable to have images of Christ and the saints. These are human beings and not the mysterious, unseen God himself. This was the argument put forward by St John of Damascus at the time of the **iconoclasts**.

> **Iconoclasts** were a movement to remove images from Churches.

However, images are not worshipped themselves; only God is worshipped. Images are respected and honoured. They help people to focus and pray or meditate as blessed objects, sacred signs and visual aids.

> Very rightly the fine arts are considered to rank among the noblest activities of man's genius, and this applies especially to religious art and to its highest achievement, which is sacred art. (*Sacrosanctumconcilium* 122)

Sculptures and statues

REVISED

Catholic religious art also allows three-dimensional images (i.e. statues and sculptures), whereas the Eastern Churches only allows two-dimensional paintings. Two common statues are ones of the Sacred Heart and of Christ on the cross (a crucifix):

- The **Sacred Heart** is a statue of Jesus and a symbol of the eternal love of God as revealed by Jesus. Jesus points to his heart, which is wounded by thorns, and fire rises and burns from within it. It is not meant to be taken literally:
  - the heart represents love
  - the thorns show that Jesus suffered for humanity
  - the fire shows the everlasting love and presence of God.
- The **crucifix** showing Jesus hanging on the cross reminds Catholics of his death and sacrifice. It reminds Catholics of his forgiveness of sins, of his love for all, even though he was cruelly treated and rejected.

Different Christian views on sculptures and images of Jesus

Protestant Christians tend to think that there is a danger that having images and sculptures of Jesus leads people to be superstitious and to worship them as idols.

- They might find the Sacred Heart rather upsetting and violent, taking it too literally, rather than as an image of the love of God.
- They may react to the crucifix by arguing that Christ is risen and not still on the cross. This is to misunderstand the symbolism, and they themselves will have readings, poems and hymns that speak of Jesus on the cross.

> Whoever venerates an image venerates the person portrayed in it. The honour paid to sacred images is a 'respectful veneration' not the adoration due to God alone. (*Catechism of the Catholic Church*, 2132)

Now test yourself

TESTED

1 What does the ICHTHUS symbol stand for?
2 What does the alpha and the omega symbol show about Catholic belief in the incarnation?
3 What is the meaning of images of the Sacred Heart? Why do some Christians find this difficult?
4 What does the crucifix remind people of, and why are some Christians opposed to using it?

Beliefs and teachings

Jesus as the incarnate Son

REVISED ☐

Incarnation literally means 'made flesh' and refers to God becoming human as Jesus.

Jesus is shown to be God incarnate in various ways in the Scriptures. St Luke and St Matthew's gospels describe the 'annunciation' which was when Mary was told by the angel Gabriel that despite being a virgin she would give birth to a baby who would be the son of God.

Luke 1:26–38 tells the story from Mary's point of view. He begins with the Annunciation as the angel greets Mary and the Holy Spirit comes upon her. She is obedient and the child she will have is to be the Son of God.

Matthew 1:18–24 tells the story of the birth and is told from Joseph's (Mary's husband) viewpoint. He was afraid and wanted to divorce Mary secretly, for a pregnancy outside of marriage was a scandal that could have you stoned. An angel tells him it is God's doing in a dream. Matthew refers to the prophecy 'a young woman shall conceive and bear a son, and shall call his name Immanuel.' (Isaiah 7:14)

Jesus as the divine Word

REVISED ☐

John's gospel starts with a description of the Word of God.

> In the beginning was the Word, and the Word was with God, and the Word was God. He was in the beginning with God; all things were made through him, and without him was not anything made that was made. In him was life, and the life was the light of men. [...]
>
> And the Word became flesh and dwelt among us, full of grace and truth; we have beheld his glory, glory as of the only Son from the Father. (John 1:1 and 1:14)

Catholics believe that the Word of God refers to Jesus and the passage from John's gospel:
- Shows Jesus, as the eternal Son, has existed along with God for all time: 'In the beginning was the Word.'
- Distinguishes between God as Father and Jesus as the eternal Son: 'The Word was with God.'
- Shows that Jesus was divine: 'the Word was God.'
- Shows that Jesus lived as a human on earth: 'The Word became flesh and made his dwelling among us.'

The Gospel of Mark describes Jesus revealing that he was the son of God through the miracles he performed and his teaching.

Jesus as fully human and divine

REVISED ☐

Jesus was not a demigod; half human and half God. Nor was he God appearing as a man in disguise, or as a man inspired by God. He was both fully God and fully man at the same time.

Somehow there was a joining of the human and the divine in Jesus, like two sides of a coin that cannot be separated.

Son of Man

Jesus is seen as fully human in the Gospels as he eats and drinks, he wept when Lazarus died, was troubled and he suffered on the cross.

Jesus is recorded in the Gospels as referring to himself as '**the Son of Man**'.

> And he began to teach them that the Son of Man must suffer many things [...] (Mark 8:31)

This could have different meanings:
- That he was an ordinary human being who suffered the same suffering and joy as any other human.
- That he is a divine figure who had control over the whole world.

Son of God

The Gospels describe the miracle of the virgin birth, other miracles performed by Jesus and Jesus' resurrection and ascension. All of which indicate he was fully God as well as fully man.

The Gospel of Mark describes how after his arrest Jesus is asked by the High Priest 'Are you the Christ, the Son of the Blessed One?' Jesus replies that he is.

'**Son of God**' was a term that had been used in the Old Testament to refer to holy or saintly people, but Catholics believe that when the term is used for Jesus it means that Jesus was God incarnate. He is seen as the most holy man, and the fullest revelation of God in a human life.

To refer to Jesus as Son of God is about God becoming incarnate, taking flesh as a human being. It was the eternal Son, the second person of the Trinity, who became incarnate. He was sent by the Father through the power of the Holy Spirit, to take on human nature for our salvation. The incarnation therefore leads us back to the Holy Trinity. The language of the Holy Trinity uses analogies of human nature and relationships to describe God's actual, mysterious nature, which is beyond our fullest abilities to understand. Catholics (and all Christians) see Jesus as fully human and fully God. There is that which is earthly and that which is divine, united in Christ.

Christians have often spoken of Jesus as 'Son of God' and 'Son of Man', referring to the divine and human natures of Jesus. 'Son of Man' has richer meanings in the Scriptures, though.

Son of God is a title that could mean a human being, a holy person, a king, and also, with Jesus, the unique Son of God, God incarnate.

Son of Man is a title that could mean a representative human being, a prophet or a cosmic saviour.

Word is God acting in the world, speaking and sending his power. Jesus is seen as the Word of God made flesh.

Now test yourself

TESTED

1 What does the beginning of John's gospel teach about Jesus?
2 What is meant by 'Son of God'?
3 What is meant by 'Son of Man'?
4 Give one way in which the gospels show that Jesus shows that he was fully human.
5 Give one way in which the gospels show that Jesus shows that he was fully divine.

Sources of authority

Jesus as the fulfilment of the law

The Old Testament describes how God gave Moses rules that people should live by including the Ten Commandments. This is what is meant by Old Testament Law. However, the Jewish people did not always live by law.

Jesus is seen as fulfilling the Old Testament Law, because he is God made man and the perfect human being (because of the incarnation). He says:

'Do not think that I have come to abolish the Law or the Prophets; I have not come to abolish them but to fulfil them.'

Jesus models the Christian virtues of faith, hope and love, helping the poor, weak and the sick.

He also gives definitive moral teachings about how people should live, in the Beatitudes and in his parables.

- The **Beatitudes** (Matthew 5:1–12) – these nine sayings, are part of the Sermon on the Mount and sum up the Christian lifestyle as taught by Jesus. Jesus tells people to remember the weak, the poor, have mercy, make peace and bless someone if they persecute you ('beatitude' comes from the Latin *beatus* to be blessed or happy). Jesus invites his followers to seek the kingdom of God and to begin to put themselves into it spiritually by changing their attitudes.

- The Sheep and the Goats (Matthew 25:31–46) this parable imagines God as a shepherd sorting out his sheep from the goats and is about how people should respond to those in need. The sheep represent people who have cared for others, and helped their neighbours, these are the people who will go to heaven. Jesus teaches that he is to be found in those who suffer and are poor and in prison.

The actions praised in the parable of the Sheep and Goats above are similar to the teaching of the Catholic Church about how people should respond to those in need:

- feeding the hungry
- giving drink to the thirsty
- welcoming strangers
- giving clothes to those who have none
- visiting the sick
- visiting those in prison
- burying the dead if people die a long way from home and any civilisation.

Blessed are the poor in spirit, for theirs is the kingdom of heaven.

Blessed are those who mourn, for they shall be comforted.

Blessed are the meek, for they shall inherit the earth.

Blessed are those who hunger and thirst for righteousness, for they shall be satisfied.

Blessed are the merciful, for they shall obtain mercy.

Blessed are the peacemakers, for they shall be called sons of God.

Blessed are the pure in heart, for they shall see God.

Blessed are those who are persecuted for righteousness' sake, for theirs is the kingdom of heaven.

Blessed are you when men revile you and persecute you and utter all kinds of evil against you falsely on my account. Rejoice and be glad, for your reward is great in heaven, for so men persecuted the prophets who were before you. (Matthew 5:1–12)

Tradition

Many early Christian writers, called the Church Fathers, wrote about the incarnation. St Irenaeus of Lugdunum (Lyon, France) wrote *Against the Heresies (Adversus Haereses)* in the second century CE. The following extract is from Book 4, Chapter 20, Section 7.

From the beginning the Son is the one who teaches us about the Father; he is with the Father from the beginning. The Word became the steward of God's grace for the advantage of men, for whose benefits he made such wonderful arrangements. The glory of God is a human being, fully alive and what brings life to a man is the vision of God. If the revelation of God through creation gives life to all who life upon the earth, much more does the manifestation of the Father through the Word give life to those who see God.

Jesus is the fullest revelation of God possible in human form.

Jesus as the Word incarnate brought grace and forgiveness.

God's glory (greatness) is seen in human beings forgiven.

Jesus brings life from God to those who trust him.

Magisterium

In the history of Christianity various beliefs have been held about Jesus including:

● that he was half man, half God
● that he was simply a very holy and spiritual man
● that he wasn't really flesh and blood but only an appearance of God.

However, the Catholic Church believes that these are incorrect and that Jesus was both fully human and fully divine.

Two recent documents sum up Church teaching about the incarnation.

● *Dei Verbum* ('God's Word') – a document published in 1965 from **Vatican II**: 'For he sent his Son, the eternal Word, who enlightens all men, so that He might dwell among men and tell them of the innermost being of God [...] Jesus Christ, therefore, the Word made flesh, was sent as "a man to men".' This explains that Jesus becoming a man was the only way for humans to truly understand God.

● *Verbum Domini* ('The Word of the Lord') – a document written by Pope Benedict XVI in 2010: 'The Son himself is the Word, the Logos: the eternal word became small – small enough to fit into the manger. He became a child, so that the word could be grasped by us. Now the word is not simply audible; not only does it have a voice, now the word has a face, one that we can see: that of Jesus of Nazareth.' This explains that Jesus' incarnation made God visible to us on earth.

> The **Beatitudes** are nine sayings in the Sermon on the Mount about being blessed or happy.
>
> **Vatican II** was the Second Vatican Council where all the Catholic bishops met with the Pope in the early 1960s.

Now test yourself

1 What are the Beatitudes?
2 Which of the Church Fathers wrote about the incarnation in *Adversus Haereses*? Quote one point he taught about Christ.
3 How does Jesus fulfil the Old Testament law?
4 How does Jesus model Christian virtues in the gospels?
5 What did Pope Benedict XVI teach about the incarnation in Verbum Domini?

Practices

Sacraments, grace and the nature of reality

Grace means a free gift of love, a blessing that we have done nothing to deserve. The word comes from *gratia* meaning gift. Christians believe that God's love, his grace, is given to all people.

They believe that there are some actions that bring God's presence and grace and these are known as the **sacraments**. St Augustine defined a sacrament as 'a visible sign of invisible grace.'

Christians believe that as creator of the world, God is present within it and it is a gift of love. Through the incarnation of God in Jesus, this takes on a fuller meaning. Catholics see that physical things can be vehicles of spiritual things. Very ordinary things can become instruments of God's love and grace, things such as water, oil, bread and wine. God uses them and comes through them.

The seven sacraments

The Catholic Church recognises seven sacraments. These are:
- Baptism
- Confirmation
- Eucharist (Holy Communion)
- Marriage
- Holy Orders
- Confession (also Penance or Reconciliation)
- Sacrament of the sick

The Catechism describes the sacraments as **efficacious** signs, this means that they do something and are not just symbolic. For example, marriage joins a husband and wife, confession brings forgiveness. These effects 'sanctify' the receiver – they make them more holy.

Sacraments have two aspects, the **matter** and the **form**. The matter is the physical thing or action; the form is the words used and their meaning. The seven were all begun (instituted) by Jesus.

Sacrament	Matter	Form	Effect
Baptism	Water	'I baptise you in the name of the Father, and of the Son, and of the Holy Spirit.'	Baptism cleanses from sin and joins the person to the Church, the body of Christ.
Confirmation	Holy oil (**chrism**)	'Be sealed with the gift of the Holy Spirit.'	Confirmation strengthens the person by the Holy Spirit.
Eucharist	Bread and wine	'The words of Jesus, "This is my body, this is my blood…"'	Eucharist brings the presence of the risen Christ in his body and blood.
Marriage	The consent of the couple	The exchange of vows	Marriage joins a couple as husband and wife.
Holy orders	The candidate	The laying on of hands by the bishop with certain words	Holy Orders makes a man a bishop, priest or deacon.
Confession	The sins of the penitent	The words of Absolution: 'I absolve you from your sins in the name of the Father, and of the Son, and of the Holy Spirit.'	Confession brings forgiveness of sins.
Sacrament of the sick	Oil	'Through this holy anointing may the Lord in his love and mercy help you with the grace of the Holy Spirit. May the Lord who frees you from sin, save you and raise you up.'	Sacrament of the sick brings forgiveness, comfort, inner strength and sometimes physical healing.

Commentaries on Exam Practice answers at **www.hoddereducation.co.uk/myrevisionnotes**

Imago Dei

Catholics and all Christians believe that human beings are made in the image of God (*imago Dei*). This means that every individual is valued and uniquely loved. For Catholics this includes unborn children. This is so from the moment of their conception in the womb. This is when an egg is fertilised by sperm. This begins life and, unless there are medical problems, will form into a baby ready to be born.

The soul is believed to be present from the moment of conception, as can be seen in the Gospel story of the Annunciation. When Mary receives the message of the angel there is a touch of life in her womb and the single cell is Jesus, growing gradually into a baby.

The Gospel of Luke describes how when Mary was pregnant with Jesus she visited her cousin Elizabeth who was pregnant, too. Elizabeth's baby 'leaped in her womb' because he recognised the presence of Jesus in Mary's womb. Catholics believe that this is evidence that Jesus was recognised as a living person from conception.

> For behold, when the voice of your greeting came to my ears, the babe in my womb leaped for joy. (Luke 1:44)

Catholic views on abortion

Catholics argue against abortion because
- They believe that every person is made in the image of God and so should be valued, this includes unborn children because life begins at conception.
- Catholics believe in protecting the weak and innocent.
- Even though a brain and organs have not yet developed, they will do, and the **zygote** has all the potential for this to happen, like a seed growing into a plant.

> From the moment of its conception life must be guarded with the greatest care while abortion and infanticide are unspeakable crimes. (*Gaudium et spes* 51)

Grace is a free gift of divine love and blessing.

Sacrament is an action and words that convey a spiritual blessing.

Efficacious means having an effect, and generally used in reference to the sacraments.

Matter is the physical or mental thing used in a sacrament.

Form are the words used when performing a sacrament.

Chrism is holy oil used at Confirmation

Imago Dei is Latin for the 'image of God'.

Zygote is a fertilised egg in the womb.

Now test yourself

1 What is meant by grace?
2 How should a sacrament be defined?
3 List the seven sacraments.
4 What is the matter and form of the sacrament of confirmation?
5 Give any two reasons why Catholics oppose abortion.

The triune god

Forms of expression – music and the glory of God

The glory of God expressed through music

The glory of God is the inexpressible splendour and mystery of God. Music is a way of expressing deep things about God, things that are beyond description in words.

Vatican II describes music as 'a treasure of inestimable value' and says that music is the highest form of art to praise God. Music:
- is evocative – it inspires thoughts and emotions
- expresses joy – Christian worship should be joyful as it celebrates the resurrection of Christ
- expresses love, as St Augustine said, 'A song is a thing of joy; more profoundly, it is a thing of love.'

Various types of music are used in worship, including:
- **psalms** – Biblical hymns and poems that express joy, repentance, sorrow, praise and love put to music
- **plainchant** or **Gregorian chant** (named after Pope Gregory) – this is chanted with voices alone (not accompanied with instruments) and often used in monasteries. It is soothing and evokes an air of mystery
- **traditional hymns** – these are hymns that have been used for a long time, they often have several verses which express some aspect of Catholic belief and a reason to praise God, such as the incarnation at Christmas. The words can sometimes seem to be old-fashioned but they can contain deep meanings and sometimes are very poetic
- **contemporary worship songs** – after Vatican II there was a new emphasis on people being more personally involved in the Mass. One way of doing this was encouraging people to sing and this led to new music being composed with more contemporary tunes such as 'Make Me a Channel of Your Peace' or 'Here I am Lord'.

Music in the Mass

Some sections of the Mass can be sung with instrumental music accompanying, these are called mass settings. These short pieces of music, or chants, emphasise certain sections and their importance. They are:
- Kyries – the 'Lord have mercy'
- Gloria – the 'Glory to God' hymn of praise
- Alleluia – this is just before the Gospel is read
- Sanctus – the 'Holy, Holy, Holy' in the Eucharistic prayer
- Eucharistic acclamations – these are short statements of faith made by the people in the Eucharistic prayer (when thanks to God is given, and bread and wine are consecrated), which otherwise is said by the priest

- Doxology – 'Through him, and with him and in him' at the end of the Eucharistic prayer
- *Agnus Dei* – 'Lamb of God' just before receiving communion.

Mass settings are used in order to highlight certain parts of the music and to draw out the meaning. They help the congregation to participate rather than just listening.

Eucharistic acclamations

REVISED

Some key meanings of the Mass can be seen in the chants and acclamations:

- The Kyries speak of mercy and the mass begins with penitence, saying sorry for sins.
- The gospel reading has a chant of 'Alleluia' to mark it out as special as it is the words and deeds of Jesus.
- The Sanctus is based upon the hymn of the angels in heaven, showing that God is present among the people.
- The *Agnus Dei* is a reminder that Jesus is present in the consecrated bread and wine, the 'Lamb of God' who died to forgive sins.

> He who sings prays twice. (St Augustine, *Catechism of the Catholic Church*, 1156)
>
> Anyone, therefore, who has learnt to love the new life has learnt to sing a new song [...] so let us love God with the love He has given us. (St Augustine, Sermon 34:1)

A **psalm** is a hymn of praise, repentance or lament.

Plainchant is the traditional settings for reciting the Psalms, using the human voice alone.

Now test yourself

TESTED

1 Why is music important in worship for Christians?
2 List four different types of Christian music.
3 Give two reasons why chants and acclamations are used during the mass.
4 In what way is the reading of the Gospel treated differently, and why?

Beliefs and teachings

The Trinity

REVISED

Christians only believe in one God; however, they also believe that God is made up of three persons: the Father, the Son and the Holy Spirit. This idea of God as a **trinity** is a central belief and mystery of the Christian faith. The Catechism states that it 'is the central mystery of Christian faith and life.' (*Catechism of the Catholic Church*, 234)

The Nicene Creed teaches the Trinity. Three of its 'I believe' statements are about the Father, the Son and the Holy Spirit:
● The Father is 'one God' who is responsible for making all things.
● The Son is 'the only begotten Son of God' who has always existed with the Father and became human to die and be resurrected to save human kind. 'Begotten' is an old English world for being born, or produced from. The idea here is that the Son is eternal, never having a beginning, but always coming forth from the Father within the life of the Trinity.
● The Holy Spirit is 'the Lord, the giver of life'.

The Catechism states:

> The Trinity is One. We do not confess three Gods, but one God in three persons. (*Catechism of the Catholic Church*, 253)

This is the great mystery for believers. How can three be one? Some people compare it to a three-leafed clover or liquid water, steam and ice all being H_2O.

The roots of the Trinity in the Scriptures

Christian understanding of God as three in one can be found in scripture:
● Deuteronomy 6:4 teaches that God is one. Catholics believe there is one God, not several, though the one God is made up of three persons: 'Hear, O Israel: The Lord our God is one Lord.'
● Matthew 3:16–17 describes the baptism of Jesus (the Son). It also talks about the other persons of the Trinity.
  ○ It describes the Spirit of God descending like a dove.
  ○ It describes the Father's voice coming from heaven.
  ○ It shows a clear belief in the Trinity.
● Galatians 4:6, one of St Paul's letters, again shows belief in the Trinity, as St Paul teaches that God sends the Spirit of his Son into the hearts of believers. 'Because you are sons, God has sent the Spirit of his Son into our hearts, crying, "Abba! Father!"'

Belief in the Trinity and Genesis

REVISED

> In the beginning God created the heavens and the earth. The earth was without form and void, and darkness was upon the face of the deep; and the Spirit of God was moving over the face of the waters.
>
> And God said, 'Let there be light,' and there was light. (Genesis 1:1–3)

Christian belief in the Trinity has influenced how they understand this passage from Genesis that describes God's creation of the world:

- The passage describes the Spirit being involved with Creation 'moving over the face of the waters.'
- God the Father brings things in to being with his Word, by ordering things to happen. Another title for Jesus, the Son, is the Word.

So Christians believe that the opening words of the Bible support belief in the Trinity.

The Trinity in Catholic life today

REVISED

The first encyclical of Pope Benedict XVI was *Deus Caritas Est*, 'God is Love'.

> The Spirit is also the energy which transforms the heart of the Church community, so that it becomes a witness before the world to the love of the Father, who wishes to make humanity a single family in his Son. The entire activity of the Church is an expression of a love that seeks the integral good of man. (Pope Benedict, *Deus Caritas* Est, 19)

Pope Benedict teaches here that the love of God is poured out in the Church by the Holy Spirit, and then should be poured out in the world. This involves caring for people, the poor and seeking peace. Catholics think of God as outgoing, giving love to all, and so the Church should also reflect this by its **mission** and **evangelisation**, going out to help others and to teach about Christ.

> The Church on earth is by her nature missionary, since, according to the plan of the Father, she has as her origin the mission of the Son and the Holy Spirit. (*Catechism of the Catholic Church*, 850)

The Catechism teaches that the mission of the Church is the same as the mission of Jesus: to show the love of the Father through the power of the Holy Spirit. Belief in the Trinity is therefore central to the existence of the Church and its mission. In a sense, the incarnation continues in the Word and the sacraments. God's love, shown in the actions of the Church, helps, challenges and transforms people facing the pain and hostility that can be in the world. Care for people in this life is important as well as preparing them for the next in Catholic belief.

> All authority in heaven and on earth has been given to me. Go therefore and make disciples of all nations, baptising them in the name of the Father and of the Son and of the Holy Spirit, teaching them to observe all that I have commanded you; and lo, I am with you always, to the close of the age. (Matthew 28:18–20)

By 'make disciples' Jesus meant baptising in the name of the Trinity and teaching the Gospel.

Trinity is one God in three equal persons of the Father, the Son and the Holy Spirit.

A **mission** is going out to spread the Word of God and to show the love of God by helping with social needs.

Evangelisation (also called evangelism) is the communication of the good news of the Gospel through preaching, teaching, media, drama or a holy life.

Now test yourself

TESTED

1 What is meant by the Trinity?
2 How is the Trinity seen in the story of the baptism of Jesus?
3 Does calling the Son 'only begotten' mean that he had a beginning?
4 Explain why belief in the Trinity helps Catholics believe in mission and evangelisation.

Sources of authority

Scripture

Catholic belief about the Trinity comes from references to the three persons of the Trinity in the Bible (although the term Trinity is never used). Two examples are:

- Mark 1:9–11 is an account of the baptism of Jesus, whereby the persons of the Trinity are present:
  - Jesus the Son is baptised by John.
  - The heavens split open and the Holy Spirit comes down like a dove.
  - The voice of the Father is heard coming from heaven.
- Galatians 4:6–7, one of St Paul's letters, also teaches about God sending the Spirit of his Son into the hearts of believers so that they are not servants but sons, and can say 'Abba', an intimate name for Father. And because you are sons, God has sent the Spirit of his Son into our hearts, crying, 'Abba! Father!' (Galatians 4:6)

God's love

The Trinity is seen by Christians as an example of the love of God in action, as the persons give themselves to each other perfectly and reach out with that love to the world.

St Augustine

St Augustine in the fifth century CE described the Trinity as a great mystery.

He argued that for love to exist there must be three parts, just like there are three parts of the trinity:

- the lover
- the beloved (the person who is loved)
- the love that binds them.

The Trinity contains all three parts. St Augustine believed that the love that unites the Trinity also flowed out in to the world to Christians.

He saw the Father as giving the gift of unity, the Son the gift of equality and the Spirit as the gift of harmony. He wrote here about the inner life of the Trinity, what is known as the *immanent* Trinity. This was his emphasis but he implied that the love of the Trinity was expressed outwards, too.

Catherine LaCugna

Catherine LaCugna was a theologian of the twentieth century. She thought that too much focus had been put on the inner workings of the Trinity and that instead we should try and understand God from what he has done in the world; his actions.

She believes that the Son comes from God and the Holy Spirit is what binds them together. God sent Jesus to earth (the incarnation) to die and be resurrected to restore human beings' relationship with God. He also sends the Holy Spirit to guide and inspire Christians. These are acts of love. LaCugna places emphasis on the external working of the Trinity, acting in the world.

Similarities and differences

Similarities between St Augustine and Catherine LaCugna	Differences between St Augustine and Catherine LaCugna
Both believe that God is love and that this love is not a static thing but constantly flowing out to humanity.	• Augustine focuses on the internal relationship of love between the persons of the Trinity. • Catherine LaCugna focuses on how God's love is shown in his outward actions towards humankind.

Conciliar magisterial authority

REVISED

- The Pope is seen as the successor of St Peter by the Catholic Church, and the bishops of the apostles. Peter was appointed to govern the Church (Matthew 16:18–19) and the apostles were promised the guidance of the Holy Spirit (John 16:13).
- Because the Pope and bishops are believed to have succeeded from the Apostles it is believed they have the authority to make decisions about Church doctrine – this is the Magisterium.
- Conciliar magisterium is when the pope and bishops come together to work out doctrine in councils.

Two **councils** have been particularly important in determining Church doctrine on the Trinity:

> **Council** is a gathering of all the bishops with the Pope.

- **Council of Nicaea** (325 CE)– This met to discuss whether Jesus was equal to God. The council concluded that Jesus was fully divine and eternal – equal to God the Father. It also made belief in the Holy Spirit central to the faith.
- **Council of Constantinople** (381 CE) – In 381 CE at Constantinople another Council was held. This council confirmed that the Holy Spirit was fully God, and the third part of the Trinity. This followed the teaching of St Basil that the Trinity is: 'one God or divine reality in the persons of the Father, and the Son and the Holy Spirit.'
- The Nicaea-Constantinople Creed (or Nicene Creed) is a statement of faith that was created and finalised in these two councils.

The infallibility promised to the Church is also present in the body of bishops, when, together with Peter's successor [the Pope], they exercise the supreme Magisterium, above all in an Ecumenical Council. (*Catechism of the Catholic Church*, 891)

I believe in the Holy Spirit, the Lord, the giver of life, who proceeds from the Father and the Son, who with the Father and the Son is adored and glorified. (Creed of Nicea-Constantinople, as adapted for use in the Catholic Mass).

Now test yourself

TESTED

1 St Augustine thought of the three parts of love as akin to the three parts of God in the Trinity. What were these?
2 St Augustine thought of each person of the Trinity as a different gift. What gifts are they?
3 What emphasis does Catherine LaCugna have in her teaching about the Trinity?
4 What did the Council of Nicaea teach about the Son and the Holy Spirit?

Practices

Baptism

Baptism is a sacrament that was established by Jesus when he instructed his disciples to baptise others:

● It is the sacrament that signals entry, or initiation, into the Catholic Church.
● In the Catholic Church babies are usually baptised, but you can be baptised at any age.
● The priest will baptise people with the following words: 'In the name of the Father, and of the Son and of the Holy Spirit.'
● Water is used to symbolise a cleansing and washing away of **original sin**, and people are reborn in to a new life with the Father, the Son and the Holy Spirit.

Prayer

The Catechism describes **prayer** as 'the raising of one's mind and heart to God.' Prayer involves setting aside some time to speak to God.

Prayer can contain different aspects such as
● adoration – showing deep love and respect for God
● thanksgiving – saying thank you to God
● repentance – saying sorry to God
● intercession – asking God to help others
● petition – asking God to help the worshipper.

Linking this with belief in the Trinity, Christians believe that the Spirit helps them to pray, through Jesus Christ and to the Father. The three are all of a piece, a sublime unity, helping, allowing and hearing our prayer.

It is not important how people pray, but that they do. There are different sorts of prayer that might be used at different times:

Type of prayer	Description	Why do people use this type of prayer?
Traditional prayer	A prayer with set words that has been used over a long time.	Familiar words that can be recited easily can bring comfort and help focus the mind on God.
Spontaneous prayer	Praying using your own words, people often feel they have been inspired by the Holy Spirit.	People can use their own words to express themselves and this can help them feel a more personal connection to God.

Postures in prayer

Human beings are not just minds but also bodies. We express a lot through our movements, or what is known as 'body language'. Prayer can be expressed in bodily postures besides words, the postures can help the worshipper focus and can reflect the intention of the prayer.

If we look at some of the intentions of prayer we can see some example of how different positions might reflect this:

Intention of prayer	How this might be reflected in the worshipper's posture
Adoration – showing deep love and respect for God Thanksgiving – saying thank you to God	Kneeling or bowing to show deep respect for God. Similarly standing to pray can indicate respect, in the same way you'd stand up to greet an important person. Hands may be slightly raised with open palms, too, to suggest being open to God.
Repentance – saying sorry to God	Lying down (prostrating) or kneeling are positions often adopted by people asking God for forgiveness as it is showing they are completely humble in front of God.
Intercession – asking God to help others Petition – asking God to help the worshipper	Joining hands is how people in prayer are often depicted. While this posture shows that the worshipper is asking God for something, it is not often used today. Perhaps more emphasis is placed upon mental prayer here, i.e. what is being asked for. People can stand, kneel or sit for this.

The only important thing about prayer is that you show up to do it! (Cardinal Basil Hume, 1923–99)

Now test yourself

TESTED

1 Why is baptism performed by pouring water three times?
2 Give a definition of prayer.
3 Describe two postures that can be used in prayer. What ideas about prayer do they show?
4 Why do some people like to use traditional prayers, and some use their own words?

Baptism is the sacrament of initiation into the Church, with water poured three times in the name of the Father, the Son and the Holy Spirit.

Original Sin is the inherited sin of Adam; of the first human beings who turned against God. This creates moral weakness and mortality.

Prayer is raising the mind to God.

Redemption

Forms of expression – architecture and design

Architecture of Catholic churches

A church building is a public place for meeting to celebrate the Eucharist (as opposed to the Church, with a capital 'C' which means all Catholics). The architecture and design of churches reflects Christian ideas about redemption – being saved through Christ.

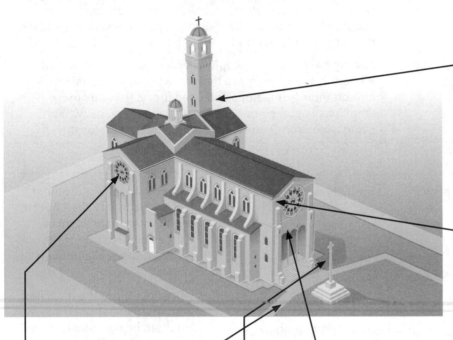

Towers and steeples represent prayer and worship rising up to heaven, a physical representation of what takes place inside the building.

It is common for churches to be cruciform in shape. This means that they are in the shape of a cross. This is to signify the importance of the death of Jesus.

Modern church buildings tend to be simpler than those that were built a long time ago. As a result of Vatican II and the changes it made to worship, some churches built since the 1960s are radically different than those that were built before. For example, some churches are circular in design with the altar in the middle. This signifies the oneness of the worshippers and that they are all sharing in the sacrificial meal at the altar. It can also stand for the eternity of God.

Traditionally, churches face towards the east as the sun rises is the east and is a reminder of the resurrection of Jesus bringing new life.

Churches are often very tall with domes or vaulted ceilings. This creates a space which is pointing up, showing a connection with God and heaven.

Very often stained glass is used in churches, usually displaying stories from the Bible or lives of the saints. Similarly inside the Church there may be the Stations of the Cross, which are images that depict the last days of Jesus' life.

Many churches have crosses both inside and outside to represent the death of Jesus. Some churches may have other statues like the sacred heart representing Jesus' suffering and love for humanity.

Features found in churches

The **lectern** is the stand from where the Bible is read. It can be simple or ornate. It is also called 'the table of the Word' as the Scriptures are read from there. This is the idea that human beings feed, metaphorically and spiritually, upon the Word of God.

The **altar** is where the Eucharist is offered and celebrated. It is the focal point of a church building. It is the altar of sacrifice, where the offering of Jesus on the cross is remembered and represented in the present. The altar is positioned in the east of the building. This is ancient custom for east is the position of the rising sun, which also symbolises the resurrection.

The **crucifix** is a central symbol in Catholic churches. It symbolises the suffering of Jesus when he died for the forgiveness of human sins, and therefore also the love of Jesus and God for humanity.

The **tabernacle** is an ornate type of safe or container for the Blessed Sacrament, the consecrated hosts from the mass. These are reserved for taking to the sick who could not come to mass and also as a focus for prayerful adoration. Catholics believe that the **Real Presence** of the risen Christ is in the sacrament and this is a powerful focus for prayer for them. To show that the **Blessed Sacrament** is kept there, a sanctuary light burns in front of the tabernacle seven days a week.

A **lectern** is the stand where the Scriptures are read out.

The **altar** is the stone table where the Eucharist is celebrated and offered.

The **crucifix** is an image of Christ on the cross.

The **tabernacle** is the ornate container for the blessed sacrament.

Real Presence is the belief that Christ is present in the consecrated bread and wine.

The **blessed sacrament** is the consecrated bread (the host) and the consecrated wine, i.e. the body and blood of Christ.

Contrasting architecture

There is some variation between features of churches between the different Christian denominations:

The altar

Catholic and Protestant beliefs about the Eucharist and Mass are different. Catholics believe that the bread and wine used in mass actually become the body and blood of Christ – so his sacrifice on the cross is re-presented (made present) every mass. This means that the altar on which this happens is central to a Catholic Church.

Protestants believe that the Mass is just a remembrance of Jesus' last supper and sacrifice. Therefore some Protestant Churches have a table instead.

Depiction of the cross and Jesus

There are differences between how different denominations choose to portray Jesus and the cross.

- Catholic churches often display a crucifix, this is a version of the cross with Jesus on. This represents God's love for humanity by depicting the suffering Jesus went through for human salvation.
- Some Protestant Christians are uneasy about the crucifix saying that Jesus did not stay on the cross, but defeated death and was resurrected. They prefer to show a plain cross rather than a crucifix.
- Other Christians feel more comfortable with artwork and statues showing the Risen Christ – Jesus after his resurrection, because it is belief in the resurrection that is the basis of the Christian faith.

Now test yourself

1 Why are some churches built in a cross shape, and why are some modern churches circular?
2 Why does every Catholic church have a crucifix on or above the altar?
3 What is the altar used for?
4 What is kept in the tabernacle and why?
5 Why do some Protestant churches have a table rather than an altar?

Beliefs and teachings

Redemption

REVISED ☐

Catholics believe that every person is born with Original Sin, which means that they have a tendency to disobey God's will. This meant that there was a broken relationship between God and humanity. Christians believe that Jesus' death on the cross restored humanity's relationship with God, but there are different interpretations about how this happened.

Restoration through sacrifice

Before Jesus, the Jews offered sacrifices of animals to atone for sins, but they had to do this frequently. The death of Jesus worked in the same way, as a sacrifice for humanity's sins. However, because Jesus is the perfect Son of God, his sacrifice was sufficient. No other sacrifice was needed. So the sacrifice of Jesus on the cross restored humanity's relationship with God.

Restoration through recreation

The Gospels describe how Jesus triumphed over death and was resurrected (brought back to life). He appeared to his disciples and many other people. The belief in the **resurrection** is central to Christian faith. The resurrection is good news for the world, for there has been a new Creation, a re-Creation. This cosmic healing includes all human beings and brings all things into harmony with the Spirit of God.

Restoration of the cosmic order

The **Ascension** is when Jesus rose back up to heaven and authority over the universe after he had defeated death and been resurrected.

The Ascension speaks of future hope, of the return of Christ and the judgement of evil. The Ascension, showing the risen Lord over all things, is a promise of the restoration of the cosmic order, or the whole universe in the sense that Jesus has not been defeated by death and sin. For Christians, he is over all creation as Lord of Lords and will have the final say of how all things work out.

> **Resurrection** is when Christ's body was transformed and he rose from the dead.
>
> **Ascension** is when Christ was taken back into heaven.
>
> **Salvation** is restoring humanity to fellowship with God.
>
> **Justification** is making someone right with God.
>
> **Eucharistic** means relating to the Eucharist, the Thanksgiving celebration where bread and wine become the body and blood of Christ.

Contrasting views of salvation

REVISED ☐

There are three basic stances regarding human beings and **salvation**. These involve grace, meaning God's mercy and love is given even when they are not deserved.

There are past, present and future ideas of grace. These are like saying 'saved, being saved and will be saved'. This suggests a beginning of forgiveness, and ongoing need for and experience of this, and a future hope for when this is complete.

Past

Some Protestant Christians tend to see salvation as totally God's doing because humans are too sinful to do anything for themselves. This is known as '**justification** by faith' as taught by Martin Luther (1483–1546) and also John Calvin (1509–64). These views stress that salvation is something that has already taken place, primarily on the cross and then in the life of the believer when they repent and become Christians.

Future

A contrasting view is that human beings can achieve their own forgiveness and salvation by their good works, as people are made in the 'image of God' (*imago Dei*). This is sometimes called 'justification by works'. This sees salvation as a future target. The problem is that this takes away the need for the death of Christ.

Past, present and future

A more Catholic or Orthodox view is to combine something of both ideas. Human beings are fallen and sinful but as they are still in the image of God they can partake in good works and kindness. They co-operate with the grace of God, which has brought forgiveness and salvation and can receive that through prayer, the Word of God and the sacraments. Salvation is something that has begun on the cross, is present in the believer and is a future goal.

Salvation and the liturgy

The Mass presents the story of redemption through Christ.
- The opening greeting and the sign of the cross is a reminder of God's presence and the mystery of the cross.
- The penitential rite is a reminder that Christians need grace and forgiveness from God.
- The story of salvation is heard in the readings form the Scriptures.
- The Gospel tells the story of Jesus.
- The **Eucharistic** Liturgy remembers the Last Supper and the death and resurrection of Jesus, leading up to giving out holy communion.
- Receiving holy communion shows that Christ accepts us and forgives us and shares his life with us.
- The Dismissal reminds people to go out and show the love of God in the world.

Now test yourself

1 Explain one way that restoration is made by Christ in Catholic belief.
2 What is meant by grace?
3 Explain what is meant by past, present and future grace.
4 Why do some Protestant only like to speak of past grace? What do they mean by 'justification by faith'?
5 Give one way in which the liturgy of the Eucharist involves the idea of redemption.

Sources of authority

Scripture

Catholic teachings about redemption are based on accounts of Jesus' life and death in the Gospels. Three examples are:

The Crucifixion in Mark 15:21–39

This account describes the death of Jesus on the cross and the darkness of sin, suffering and the belief in forgiveness. The key things this teaches about redemption are:
- Jesus was victorious over death itself, symbolised by the darkness that fell when he died.
- Jesus' death opened the way for humans to come into relationship with God, symbolised by the veil in the Temple splitting in two.

The Resurrection in John 20:1–16

The account describes one scene from the story of the resurrection of Jesus. Mary Magdalene meets the risen Christ. The key things this teaches about redemption are:
- The resurrection is authentic, historical fact. The account of a woman being the first to see the risen Christ would not have been expected in the culture, and so would not have been made up as a story.
- Some disciples visit the empty tomb and start to believe. The resurrection brought faith and starts to change people.
- All of humanity can be restored by encountering the risen Christ. This is shown by Mary in the garden, symbolic of a second Eve in the Garden of Eden.

- A renewed humanity is brought about by the resurrection. This is shown by Christ's glorious resurrection body.

The Ascension in Acts 1:6–11

This account describes the Ascension of Jesus as he returns to the glory of heaven. The key things this teaches about redemption are:
- The Holy Spirit will come to those who believe in Jesus after his ascension.
- Jesus is living now in the presence of the Father. Having overcome death and sin, he reigns as Lord.
- There is revelation and hope as the two angels tell the disciples that Jesus will return in glory.

Pentecost in Acts 2:1–4

This account describes the coming of the promised Holy Spirit. The key things this teaches about redemption are:
- The Holy Spirit gives believers faith and boldness. This is shown by the disciples gathering in a house, confused and afraid, but emerging full of faith and belief in the resurrection of Christ.
- The Holy Spirit who comes to believers is God himself. The wind and the fire are symbolic in the Bible of an appearance of God.
- The Holy Spirit brings the disciples courage to go out and witness.

Tradition

St Irenaeus (died 202 CE) had a particular way of understanding the redemption that Jesus brought; it is called the **recapitulation** theory and his argument was:
- He believed Adam had not followed God's will – he had eaten the fruit of the tree when God had forbidden it. This had led all humanity to go astray.
- Jesus was the new Adam, this was possible because he was the incarnate son of God.
- Jesus led a perfect life, always obeying God. His life was a victory over sin and his resurrection was a victory over death.
- Jesus was the new leader of the human race and because he lived a perfect life people who follow him can be saved from sin.

St Anselm (1033–1109) had a different interpretation of salvation. It is called the satisfaction theory of atonement, and his argument was:

- That by sinning humanity had dishonoured God.
- God is just and someone had to pay the price of human sin.
- By living the perfect life and sacrificing himself on the cross, Jesus paid the price, or 'ransom', for human sin. He offered 'satisfaction' for human dishonour of God.

> [...] in His work of recapitulation Christ summed up all things [...] in order that, as our species went down to death through a vanquished man, so we may ascend to life again through a victorious one [...] (St Irenaeus, *Adversus Haereses* 5.21.1)

Commentaries on Exam Practice answers at **www.hoddereducation.co.uk/myrevisionnotes**

Magisterium

Conscience is an inner moral compass. This is partly seen as the inner voice of God's guidance and is stronger and clearer for those who are redeemed by Christ. Catholic teaching says that all are bound to follow this.

Conscience must be informed by church teaching, and by finding out all the facts pertinent to a given situation. All of the redeemed must let their actions be informed by their consciences as they relate to one another.

Gaudium et Spes

Gaudium et Spes is a document from Vatican II. Section 16 speaks about conscience. It says that conscience summons people to love good and not evil. It is written into human hearts and gives human beings a dignity.

The *Catechism of the Catholic Church*

The Catechism teaches that no one must be forced to act against their conscience. The Catechism admits that in some situations it is very hard to work out what is right, but there are always guidelines that apply in every case:
- Never do evil so that good will result.
- Follow the **Golden Rule**, 'Whatever you wish that men would do to you, do so to them.' (Matthew 7:12)
- Always respect others.

> For man has in his heart a law written by God; to obey it is the very dignity of man; according to it he will be judged. Conscience is the most secret core and sanctuary of a man. There he is alone with God, Whose voice echoes in his depths. (*Gaudium et Spes*, 16)

Different Christian understandings of conscience

- Some Protestants may value their individual conscience more highly than Church tradition when considering how to interpret the Bible.
- Extreme Fundamentalists have no room for personal conscience but follow only literal rules from the Bible.
- Liberal Christians see conscience as being informed by social and family ideas, which can be challenged. Here, the example of Christ is the touchstone of morality. Love is the driving force of a true conscience for them.

Recapitulation is the idea that Christ was the new Adam who restored humanity to fellowship with God.

Conscience is the inner voice or sense of what is right and wrong.

The **Golden Rule** is to do to others what you would want to be done to yourself.

Now test yourself

1 State two ways in which Mark's account of the crucifixion teaches redemption.
2 State two ways in which John's account of the resurrection shows a belief in redemption.
3 Why does the Ascension story suggest future redemption?
4 What did St Anselm teach about ransom and satisfaction?
5 What does the Catholic Church teach about the importance of and the use of conscience?

Practices – Eucharist and Redemption

Source and summit

Catholic teaching says that the Mass or Eucharist, with consecrated bread and wine and the sharing of Holy Communion, is 'the source and summit of the Christian life.' The Mass is based upon redemption through Christ, and it restores humanity's relationship with God. It contains the whole story of salvation in Christ.

- The Eucharist is known as a saving mystery or the **paschal** mystery. It is about the saving action of Christ and the paschal term refers back to the Jewish Passover meal which remembers the liberation of the Hebrews from slavery.
- Catholics speak of the **Real Presence** of Christ in the Eucharist as the bread and the wine are transformed into the Body and Blood of Christ. It is more than a symbol.
- The Eucharist is a sacrifice, an offering of praise and also a re-presentation of the death on the cross. They are not trying to re-sacrifice Christ though. They are bringing the one sacrifice and its power into the present.
- The Mass ends with the dismissal, the *missa* in Latin. The people are sent out to take the saving message of Christ into the world.

> **Paschal** is to do with the Passover and also Easter, the Christian Passover.
>
> **Real Presence** is the belief that the bread and the wine really change in to the body and blood of Christ.
>
> **Words of Institution** is

Catholic and Other Christian views

Different Christian denominations have different views on the meaning of the Eucharist:

- **Catholics** understand the Eucharist as a sacrament, and as more than a symbol. Christ is really present as the bread and wine are changed in to his body and blood. This change is called 'transubstantiation'. The visible form of bread and wine remains, but the invisible substance, what it really is, is different.
- **Orthodox Christians** have very similar views to Catholics. The Eucharist is central to their liturgy and the real presence of Christ brings human beings into the glory and presence of God. They do not define how the change occurs though.
- **Protestant Christians** see the Eucharist as deeply meaningful but as just symbolic, a commemoration of what Jesus did. They are hesitant about any idea of repeating the sacrifice on the cross as this happened once and for all.
- **Anglicans** have a variety of views. 'High Church' Anglicans are close to the Catholic view and liturgy; 'Low Church' Anglicans are more Protestant in their views, seeing the Eucharist as a symbol with the only real presence being in the heart of the believer.

Words of Institution

The **Words of Institution** are the words the priest speaks over the bread and wine. They are the words that were spoken by Jesus at the last supper:

'This is my Body [...] This is my Blood.'

When the priest says these words Catholics believe that the bread and wine become the body and blood of Christ.

The Real Presence

The Real Presence refers to the Catholic belief that the bread and wine used in the Eucharist actually becomes the body and blood of Christ when they are consecrated. So Christ is really present in the Eucharist – it is not just symbolic.

The Real Presence of Christ is linked to the idea of sacrifice in the Mass because the Risen Jesus brings the saving power of his death on the cross into the present.

The Real Presence also encourages **eucharistic adoration** where consecrated bread, the Body of Christ, is placed in the tabernacle or displayed upon the altar and is a focus for people's prayer.

> **Eucharistic adoration** is praying before the Blessed Sacrament.

Agnus Dei

The Agnus Dei means 'Lamb of God' and this term forms part of a prayer in the liturgy.

It is reference to the Passover, when God told Jewish families in Egypt to sacrifice a lamb and put its blood on their door posts to spare their first born children from death. John the Baptist referred to Jesus as the Lamb of God, because in the same way the sacrifice of the lamb had saved the Jews in Egypt, Jesus' sacrifice saved humanity from its sins.

Now test yourself

TESTED

1 How is the Mass understood as a sacrifice by Catholics?
2 What is the word 'mass' based upon in the Eucharistic liturgy?
3 What is eucharistic adoration and why do Catholics believe that they should do this?
4 What is meant by the 'Words of Institution'?
5 What do Protestant Christians believe about the Real Presence?

Church and the Kingdom of God

Forms of expression – drama and the faith journey

The pilgrim people

REVISED

Catholics see the members of the Church as a pilgrim people, on a journey of faith towards their Heavenly Father.

The stations of the cross

There can be forms of enacted prayer, forms of drama, that help to emphasise the pilgrim nature of the Church.

The **stations of the cross** is a form of dramatic prayer as people are invited to move around the church looking at images of Jesus on his path to the cross. Prayers and short meditations are said at each one, as well as Bible readings. The moving around from station to station reflects the **pilgrimage** or journey of the life of faith, following Christ and yearning for heaven. There are either fourteen (traditionally) or fifteen stations. A station is simply a place to stop, like in a railway station, and pray.

> The **stations of the cross** are a series of 14 or 15 stations consisting of pictures of Jesus' journey to the cross.
>
> A **pilgrimage** is a journey to a holy place to pray.

1 Jesus is condemned to death.
2 Jesus carries his cross.
3 Jesus falls for the first time.
4 Jesus meets his mother.
5 Simon helps Jesus carry his cross.
6 Veronica wipes the face of Jesus.
7 Jesus falls for the second time.
8 Jesus meets the women of Jerusalem.
9 Jesus falls for a third time.
10 Jesus is stripped of his clothes.
11 Jesus is nailed to the cross.
12 Jesus dies on the cross.
13 Jesus is taken down from the cross.
14 Jesus is laid in the tomb.
15 (Sometimes added) Jesus rises from the dead.

Pilgrimage

Christians have gone on pilgrimage to holy places since the earliest days of the Church. Pilgrimage involves a journey which reflects the journey of life and of faith. It can contain special prayers, symbols and actions. Pilgrimage can involve penance (giving things up) and confession; taking time out to put things right.

- **Jerusalem** – This is a place of pilgrimage for Jews, Christians and Muslims. For Christians, it is the place where Jesus was crucified and rose again.
- **Rome** – This is where St Peter, one of the apostles, was martyred and buried. St Peter's Basilica contains his tomb and people come to pray there. It is also where the Pope lives.

- **Walsingham** – In 1061 in Norfolk, the Lady Richeldis had a vision of the Virgin Mary. Mary asked Lady Richeldis for the Holy House to be built in Walsingham. This was to be a replica of Mary's house in Nazareth. Pilgrims travelled here widely in the Middle Ages until the Reformation closed the shrine. There are now two shrines in Walsingham, one Catholic and one Anglican.
- **Lourdes** – In 1858, Bernadette, a young girl, had a vision of the Virgin Mary in a small cave (grotto) in Lourdes, France. A spring of water was found at the spot and pilgrims were told to come for healing. Many pilgrims visit each year, and disabled and sick pilgrims are cared for. There are many stories of being healed and helped by prayers there.

Drama and evangelisation

Evangelisation is the spreading of the gospel message, through words, teaching, preaching or compassionate actions. Mission is the work of spreading the gospel in these various ways, and often involves people being amongst those they are trying to influence, giving up a great deal to speak and work with them.

Films and stories can show aspects of the gospel at work in people's lives. Two examples are *The Mission* and *Les Misérables*:

- *The Mission* – This film was made in 1986 and is about the slave trade in South America and the work of the Jesuit missionaries there. A slave trader kills his stepbrother and seeks forgiveness. He finds this by being shown mercy by the native tribes whom he had taken slaves from. The Jesuits work with him among the native people, winning their respect. When ordered to abandon these tribes by the bishops for political reasons, they refuse. They follow their consciences and are killed alongside the people they were trying to serve. This film is about evangelisation, mission and showing love in action. It also shows the importance of conscience.
- *Les Misérables* – This is a novel by Victor Hugo, completed in 1862. A convict out on parole, Valjean, steals silver from a bishop. He is caught and tells the authorities that the silver was a gift; despite this being a lie, the bishop supports his story. Valjean is touched by this example of love. He changes his ways and uses the money to build a factory to provide work for others. Valjean breaks his parole and is pursued by his former jailer, Javert. Valjean has the opportunity to kill Javert, but refuses to kill his enemy. This story is about mercy and forgiveness, even to enemies. It is also an excellent example of how mission and evangelisation can involve great self-sacrifice and working with people very different from the missionaries.

> Preach the Gospel and, if you need to, use words. (Reportedly the words of St Francis of Assisi)

> The production and showing of films that have value as decent entertainment, humane culture or art, especially when they are designed for young people, ought to be encouraged and assured by every effective means. (*Inter mirfica*, 14)

Now test yourself

TESTED

1 What are the stations of the cross about, and how many are there, traditionally?
2 What does pilgrimage involve and how does this reflect an aspect of faith and human life?
3 Choose two from the list: Jerusalem, Rome, Walsingham, Lourdes. Why are these places of pilgrimage?
4 What moral and spiritual points can be found in either *The Mission* or *Les Misérables*?

Beliefs and teachings

The kingdom of God

The Lord's Prayer (or Our Father) asks that God's kingdom will come.

The **kingdom of God**, (or the reign of God) is often referred to by Jesus in the Gospels. The kingdom is about peace and wholeness where God's presence is fully with humanity. The coming of the kingdom is understood by the gospels as a gradual process, the kingdom:

● is among people or within them
● came more fully at the cross and resurrection as sins were forgiven and death was defeated. The kingdom comes to people, within, through the gift of the Holy Spirit at Pentecost
● will come in its fullness at the end of time.

Catholic beliefs about the kingdom of God are reflected in the Lord's Prayer in various ways:

● The prayer asks for the kingdom to come on earth as in heaven.
● The request for daily bread is asking for welfare, health and sharing. This is an important aspect of what people mean by 'the kingdom of God'. It is about **justice** and peace for all.
● Forgiveness is part of the life of the kingdom.
● Deliverance from evil is a mark of the kingdom, where peace and justice reigns.

> Our Father who art in heaven, hallowed be thy name. Thy kingdom come. Thy will be done on earth, as it is in heaven. Give us this day our daily bread, and forgive us our trespasses, as we forgive those who trespass against us, and lead us not into temptation, but deliver us from evil.

> When we pray, 'Thy kingdom come', we call for Christ to come again, as he promised, and for God's reign, which has already begun here on earth, to prevail definitively. (*YouCat*, 520)

Catholic teaching on justice, peace and reconciliation as signs of the kingdom

Catholics believe that the kingdom of God covers many things, including social justice and actions between people, besides spiritual matters. These actions are then 'signs of the kingdom' pointing to its nature and its values.

● Peace is not possible without justice. If people are treated unfairly and lack, then they will not be at peace.
● Peace is a sign of the kingdom. Jesus said, 'Blessed are the peacemakers, for they will be called sons of God.' (Matthew 5:9).
● Reconciliation is peace being made between two people or groups, rather than one side forgiving and the other not accepting it. Such reconciled peace is a sign of the kingdom. It reflects the sacrifice of Christ on the cross to reconcile the world to God.
● Social justice is applying peace and justice to human society, how people live together and their rights. This includes helping the poor. Pope Leo XIII wrote about social justice in *Rerum novarum* (*Concerning new things*) in 1891. He argued that employers should treat their workers fairly. Other Popes have written since about social justice, concerning workers' rights, developmental issues and warfare. This is known as Catholic social teaching.

> The **kingdom of God** is the 'Reign of God': healing, peace and justice on earth.
>
> **Justice** means fairness to all.

The hierarchy of the Church and its consultative nature

REVISED

The Catholic Church has a hierarchy of the Pope, the bishops, the priests and the people. When the Pope and all the bishops assemble together specially, this is a Council of the Church. A council carries great authority as a common mind about certain issues is reached.

Second Vatican Council (Vatican II)

This was a Council of bishops that met between 1962–65 over four sessions. It was started by Pope John XXIII and completed by Pope Paul VI. Pope John wanted to open the Church up to change, and two key phrases were **aggiornamento** (updating) and **ressourcement** (going back to the roots). Many things in the Church were ready for change. There were four main documents that were produced from the Council:

- *Dei verbum* (*The Word of the Lord*) – This document set out the relationship between [content missing?]. It said they were each inspired by the Holy Spirit and had authority for the Church. It emphasised the importance of proper Bible scholarship; studying the Bible including its literary style and the context in which it was written. Catholics were encouraged to read the Bible for themselves and learn more about it rather than just listening to it in mass.
- *Sacrosanctum concilium* (*Constitution on Sacred Liturgy*) – This document established that the liturgy of the mass needed to be more readily understood by the people and they needed to be more involved. This led to the mass being translated from Latin into the local language. The involvement of the people was a sign of the Kingdom.
- *Gaudium et spes* (*Constitution on the Church in the Modern World*) – This document said that the Church needed to be involved with the world and not separate from it. It encouraged its members to work for social justice and to be a source of 'joy and hope' to the world. Social justice and working for the betterment of humanity is a sign of the kingdom.
- *Lumen gentium* (*Constitution on the Church*) – Before the council, it was often assumed that only priests and/or monks and nuns would preach and be missionaries. This document said that every member of the Church was to be involved in the mission of the Church. Charitable groups such as CAFOD came about as a result. This mission and involvement was a sign of the kingdom.

The work of the Council shows how the hierarchy, the bishops and the Pope, need to consult with the people to help them to make decisions and to lead. (There were representatives from other Christian denominations, too, and lay people who were theological experts, but these people were in the minority.)

> The college or body of bishops has no authority unless it is understood together with the Roman Pontiff [the Pope], the successor of Peter as its head. (*Lumen gentium*, 22)

> **Aggiornamento** means updating.
>
> **Ressourcement** is going back to the sources, or original ideas.

Now test yourself

TESTED

1. Define 'the kingdom of God'.
2. Explain the stages in which Christians believe that the kingdom comes on earth.
3. What is meant by Catholic social teaching? Give one example from the writings of Pope Leo XIII.
4. List the names of the four documents of Vatican II and write one sentence for each, summing up what they are about.
5. What is meant by *aggiornamento*?

Sources of authority

Scripture

REVISED

Mary is a sign of the kingdom

Catholics believe that Mary, mother of Jesus, is a model of the Church. This means that she modelled the qualities to be a good Catholic, including being the greatest example of **discipleship**:

- Mary was a faithful disciple who responded to the message of the angel that she was to give birth to Jesus willingly.
- Mary had complete faith in God and in Jesus, she served God and never questioned God's will.
- She was one of a few of Jesus' followers to follow him right to the foot of the cross.
- She showed kindness and compassion and gave her whole life to God.

> **Discipleship** is to follow Christ and to learn his ways.
>
> The **Magnificat** is Mary's song in Luke's gospel.

The Magnificat

The Gospel of Luke describes Mary singing the **Magnificat**, which praises God. This is still used in Catholic services today. It said that the poor and the humble will be blessed more than the rich and the powerful. It is about God's salvation and also about social justice.

> My soul magnifies the Lord,
> and my spirit rejoices in God my Saviour,
> for he has regarded the low estate of his handmaiden.
>
> For behold, henceforth all generations will call me blessed;
> for he who is mighty has done great things for me,
> and holy is his name.
>
> And his mercy is on those who fear him from generation to generation.
>
> He has shown strength with his arm,
> he has scattered the proud in the imagination of their hearts,
> he has put down the mighty from their thrones,
> and exalted those of low degree;
> he has filled the hungry with good things,
> and the rich he has sent empty away.
>
> He has helped his servant Israel,
> in remembrance of his mercy,
> as he spoke to our fathers,
> to Abraham and to his posterity for ever.
> (Magnificat, Luke 1:46–55)

The Church aims to engage in the same level and spirit of social justice. The Magnificat can be seen as a controversial and radical prayer, wanting change and social justice.

The four marks of the Church

REVISED

The Nicene Creed identifies four marks, or distinguishing qualities, of the Church. The four marks of the Church are:

- **one** – there is one people of God and one Christ. This does not mean that every Catholic is the same, but that they are all united
- **holy** – though its members are far from perfect, every member of the Church has been called to holiness. This means that through baptism, a Catholic has been freed from original sin, filled with God's grace, and become a member of the holy People of God
- **catholic** – worldwide
- **apostolic** – based upon the teaching of the apostles; these were the 12 men he called to follow him.

Apostolic succession

Catholics believe that Jesus Christ founded the Church and gave his authority to his apostles, who were the 12 men he called to follow him. He gave special authority to St Peter, the leader of the apostles, to act as his representative on earth. Peter was the first pope. Catholics believe that the authority of the apostles has been handed down to the current pope and bishops. This is called **apostolic succession**.

This link to the apostles means that the pope and bishops have the authority to make decisions on points of doctrine. The teachings of the pope and bishops is called the Magisterium.

> **Apostolic succession** is the line of bishops from the first apostles, and the teaching that they handed down.

Magisterium

REVISED

The Magisterium is the teaching authority of the Church and it is formed of the pope and the bishops working together. There is the Conciliar Magisterium and Pontifical Magisterium.

The Conciliar Magisterium

Councils of the Church happen when the Pope calls all the bishops together to decide matters of doctrine or practice. Examples of Church councils include Vatican II in 1962 that looked at the Church's relationship with the modern world and the Council of Trent (1545–63) defined transubstantiation as a doctrine of the Church.

Synods are smaller scale Councils with fewer people meeting, such as the 2015 Synod on family life.

Pontifical (papal) Magisterium

The Pope has authority because he is the successor of St Peter. The Pope gives out regular teachings (ordinary magisterium) in his letters to Catholic diocese (encyclicals). However, very rarely, a Pope will make an *ex cathedra* declaration on a matter of faith and morals. When the Pope speaks *ex cathedra* (from the chair of St Peter) he seals a teaching as set and true and without error (infallible). This is very restricted and normally follows extensive consultation with all the bishops on matters of doctrine.

Catholic social teaching

Catholic social teaching is an application of the teachings of the Gospel with the needs of society and tries to influence political decisions for justice and peace.

Two examples of Catholic Social Teaching being promoted by the Magisterium are *Gaudium et spes* 1 and in *Evangelii gaudium* 53–54.

- *Gaudium et spes* says that the needs of humanity are the needs of the Church and none should be ignored. Speaking of the followers of Christ: 'Indeed nothing genuinely human fails to raise an echo in their hearts.'
- *Evangelii gaudium* attacks aspects of capitalism and a culture of prosperity where people seek material wealth and social needs are neglected.

> The culture of prosperity deadens us; we are thrilled if the market offers us something new to purchase. In the meantime all those lives stunted for lack of opportunity seem a mere spectacle; they fail to move us. (Pope Francis, *Evangelii gaudium*, 54)

Now test yourself

TESTED

1 Give one way that Mary is a sign of the kingdom.
2 Sum up the teaching of the Magnificat in two sentences.
3 What are the four marks of the Church?
4 What is meant by apostolic succession?
5 What is the difference between the Conciliar Magisterium and the Papal Magisterium?

Practices – the Church as the body of Christ

The Church is called the body of Christ and all the people in the Church make up this body.

Catholic agencies

Jesus taught that 'you should love your neighbour' and demonstrated care for the vulnerable throughout his life. Catholics put Jesus' command into action today in many ways including establishing various agencies which work as charities in the UK and internationally. Examples are:

- **DePaul UK** was set up in 1989 and named after St Vincent de Paul, who was known for his works of charity. It works with people who are homeless and has headquarters in Newcastle that can house 13 people and has 24 hour staffing. Local groups and centres exist through the country. In 2015, they supported 3,000 young people.
- **CAFOD (Catholic Agency for Overseas Development)** began in 1960 to help raise money for a mother and baby centre in Dominica, but the Bishops of England and Wales adopted the charity as the official Catholic aid agency. CAFOD now supports work with poverty and injustice in more than 30 countries. They partner with local groups and help them, for example, in El Salvador they help young people affected by gangs via the Sisters of St Clare.

> **CAFOD** is the Catholic Agency for Overseas Development.

Kingdom values

Kingdom values are justice and peace for all, seeking **reconciliation**, where possible and social justice. Love should overcome conflict.

Vocation is understood by Catholics in relation to the priesthood, family, religious life and community.

> **Reconciliation** is to make peace between two people, and to forgive.
>
> **Vocation** is a sense of calling, a specific calling to a way of life.

Priesthood

Some are called to holy orders, trained and ordained by the Bishop. Only men can be ordained in the Catholic Church. They are usually single and celibate in the Catholic Church. The gift of their lives and their service to the Gospel is a sign of kingdom values.

Family

Married people have a vocation and they take vows to be faithful to one another in the marriage service. As parents, they are called 'the domestic Church' where the family is cared for. Commitment (fidelity) and care for the family are seen as important kingdom values.

Religious life

This means that a person commits themselves to a religious community, a monastery or a convent. They take vows of poverty, chastity and obedience. Monks and nuns belong to different orders such as the Benedictines or the Poor Clares. These are enclosed orders where people stay within their monasteries or convents, praying and serving guests. Such self-giving and service reflect kingdom values of compassion for others.

Community

The Catholic Church is a community, and most people experience this in their own parishes. People can serve in groups such as the St Vincent de Paul Society (SVP) or Life, aiding the unborn and single mothers. People can also help in the parish community as special ministers of the Eucharist, or catechists preparing adults for baptism or young people for their first Holy Communion. Serving and relating to others, looking after their needs and helping their faith to grow reflect kingdom values of service, love and faithfulness.

Justice, peace and reconciliation

REVISED

Pope Francis is an example of one important Catholic who demonstrates the values of justice, peace and reconciliation. He was born Jose Mario Bergoglio in 1936 in Buenos Aires in Argentina. He was ordained priest in 1969 after entering the religious order of the Jesuits in 1958. He became Archbishop in 1998 and pope in 2013.

Justice

As Archbishop, Pope Francis sent more priests into the poorest areas of Buenos Aires. As Pope he uses the same metal cross as when Archbishop rather than a gold one. He lives in a flat in a guesthouse in Rome rather than the Papal apartments. His actions show humility and a simplicity of life, which are Kingdom values. He speaks out against economic systems that promote injustice.

Peace

Pope Francis helped restore good relations between the USA and Cuba in 2014–15. He has met leaders of countries who are opposed to each other, such as the Israeli and Palestinian presidents together. He sheltered people who were threatened by the Argentinian government in the 1970s.

Reconciliation

Pope Francis visits a local prison each Maundy Thursday and washes the feet of twelve prisoners. He has met with Jews and Muslims, and has welcomed other Christian denominations by kneeling down and asking them to pray for him.

> Through baptism Christ has made us into a kingdom of 'priests to his God and Father' (Revelations 1:6). Through the universal priesthood, every Christian is called to work in the world in God's name and bring blessings and grace to it.' (*YouCat*, 259)

Now test yourself

TESTED

1 Select one Catholic agency and explain how this tries to fulfil the command to 'Love your neighbour.'
2 How does choosing the religious life show a sign of the kingdom?
3 In what way can family life be seen as a sign of the kingdom?
4 Explain a way in which Pope Francis has supported justice, and a way he has supported peace?

Eschatology: Christian life, death and eternity

Forms of expression – artefact and eschatology

Eschatology is about the final things, the end time, death, judgement, **heaven** and **hell**. This section explores artefacts and rites that reflect these beliefs.

> **Eschatology** is what happens at the end time.
>
> **Heaven** is eternal joy in the presence of God.
>
> **Hell** is total separation from God.

The paschal candle

REVISED

The **paschal candle** is used and lit for the first time at the Easter vigil on the evening of Holy Saturday. This is the first mass of Easter which celebrates the resurrection of Jesus. It is known as 'paschal' as it is linked with Easter, which in turn, is derived from the Jewish Passover.

During the vigil:
- The candle is carried into the dark church as 'Christ our light' is said or sung three times. The people light hand candles from this. The flame represents the light of Christ which the darkness has not extinguished.
- As it is placed on its stand, a long and beautiful hymn of praise is sung, the Exultet.

> The **paschal candle** is the Easter candle lit at the first mass of Easter.

The paschal candle is also used throughout the year at baptisms when it is used to bless the water of baptism by lowering it into the font. This also symbolises the gift and hope of eternal life.

The paschal candle has several symbols on it that reflect Catholic beliefs:
- The alpha and the omega images on the candle represent the first and the last, as Jesus who was in the beginning and lasts for ever.
- The five studs pressed into the cross image represent the five wounds of Christ that he sustained when he was crucified.

Michelangelo's *The Last Judgement*

REVISED

Michelangelo painted *The Last Judgement* on the wall of the Sistine Chapel in Rome. It shows the end time when Christ comes to judge everyone and it depicts the 'four last things' in Christian tradition, death, judgement, heaven and hell:
- death – the artist has painted crowds of people in this scene, suggesting that death comes to everyone, rich and poor alike.
- judgement – Christ returns and the righteous who will go to heaven are on his right, and the damned who will go to hell are on his left. Mary, who sits next to Jesus, looks apprehensive and distressed when she looks to her left
- heaven – St Michael reads from the Book of Life and the righteous ascend into heaven. Some of the saints carry signs of their martyrdom and torture. The vision of God is a comfort and blessing.
- hell – the condemned listen as another angel reads from the Book of Death while devils try to seize them and drag them down.

Memorials

Tombstones

Graves have been around churches for generations, either under the floor or around the grounds. Tombstones mark these, sometimes with Christian symbols, a prayer or Bible verses. The common abbreviation, R.I.P. stands for 'rest in peace'. This shows a hope in eternal life. The proximity of graves to the church shows a link with the Christian faith in resurrection. The departed and the living are linked in what is known as the communion of saints.

Monuments

Sometimes monuments are built to mark graves, for example, in the early days of Christianity people were often buried in, large decorated coffins called **sarcophagi**, which were decorated with scenes of Jesus from the New Testament. The image of Jesus as the Good Shepherd was often used, showing Jesus gathering souls of the dead and leading them to heaven. Other images were also used such as a vine representing life.

> **Sarcophagi** are decorated stone tombs used by some early Christians.

Remembrance gardens

The Catholic Church did not allow cremation until 1966 out of concern for the need for the body to rise again. The nature of the resurrection is beyond physical flesh and blood, though, and the Church having rethought this, allows cremation. Now when a Catholic is cremated the ashes are buried in memorial gardens, usually near to the church building and trees or shrubs often mark the site of burial, with simple plaques remembering the departed.

Burial and cremation, with memorial gardens, show respect for the departed by not simply ignoring their bodies and memory. For Christians, this is also about the hope of heaven, as the deceased is believed to live on in eternity.

> Eternal rest grant unto them, O Lord, and let perpetual light shine upon them. May they rest in peace. Amen (Eternal Rest – a prayer for the dead)

Now test yourself

1 Give two ways the paschal candle reflects Catholic views about the Resurrection.
2 Give two ways Michelangelo's *The Last Judgement* depicts Catholic views about life after death.
3 Explain two ways Catholic beliefs about life after death are expressed in memorials.
4 Explain two ways Catholic beliefs about life after death influence funeral ceremonies.

Beliefs and teachings

The resurrection

Belief in the resurrection of Christ shaped Christian views about eschatology. St Paul believed that he had encountered the risen Christ on the road to Damascus (Acts 9:3–6). In 1 Corinthians 15 St Paul lays out central Christian beliefs about resurrection.

Christians believe that Jesus triumphed over death, which means that they too can live on after death and spend eternity with God.

Jesus' physical body was raised from the dead. This means that Catholics believe in bodily resurrection – they believe that it is not just their souls that will resurrected, but that they will be given a heavenly body. St Paul uses the image of a seed that is broken open so a plant can grow to illustrate beliefs about resurrection. This is akin to the death of the physical body (the seed) so a new, spiritual life can begin (the plant).

The four last things

Catholic beliefs about life after death are made up of the four last things:

Death

This is a letting go, a departure, a handing back of the gift of life to the Creator. Catholics don't believe that death is the end but is just the end of a person's earthly body.

Judgement

Catholics believe that after death people will be judged by God and that this **judgement** will determine what happens to them for the rest of eternity. The idea is that people face up to who they really are and what they have done, in the presence of God. Some are ready to enter God's mercy and heaven. Some need to be cleansed and healed before they are ready. Some utterly turn away from God and reject his ways.

Catholics believe in two types of judgement:
- **particular judgement** – when, after death, God makes an immediate personal judgement of how a person has behaved during their lives
- **final judgement** – Catholics believe that at the end of time Jesus will judge the whole of the world.

> **Judgement** is when God reveals the hearts of people and they are exposed to the light of his love
>
> **Particular judgement** is the individual judgement of the departed soul.
>
> **Final judgement** is when God judges the world at the end of time.
>
> **Purgatory** is a state of cleansing and healing after death to prepare the soul to enter heaven.

Heaven

Catholics believe that death is not the end, but that after death they will go on to spend eternity with God. This is what they call heaven. The experience of heaven is sometimes known as the 'beatific vision', the beautiful and blessed vision of God in his raw presence, light and love. It is not seen as static but exciting, moment by moment. St Paul states that it is beyond human imagination (1 Corinthians 2:9).

Catholics believe that some people need to be cleansed of their sins before they can enter heaven. This state of cleansing and healing is known as **purgatory**. There is a long Christian tradition of praying for the dead, when people offer prayers for those in purgatory.

> Heaven is the endless moment of love [...] Hell is the condition of everlasting separation from God, the absolute absence of love. (*YouCat* 158, 161)

Hell

Catholics believe that people who deliberately separate themselves from God and don't repent, choose not to receive God's love. They are like a bucket with a lid on that cannot receive water that someone tries to pour into it. After death, these people will be separated from God for all eternity and this is what Catholics mean by hell. There are various symbols of hell, burning fire, terrifying devils and darkness. It is chaos and destruction, not life and blessing.

> God does not damn men. Man himself is the one who refuses God's merciful love and voluntarily deprives himself of (eternal) life by excluding himself from communion with God. (*YouCat*, 162)

Different Christian beliefs about life after death

REVISED

There are contrasting beliefs about the four last things among various Christian groups:

- **Death** – Catholics believe in bodily resurrection, the soul living in a new body. Some Christians play this down, only speaking of the survival of the soul such as in near-death experiences when people feel that they leave their body briefly.
- **Final judgement** – there are various views on this, particularly among more liberal Christians, who stress the love of God, so sorrow for sins after departing life will be taken into account. The idea of a final judgement is understood as a personal and final encounter with the healing love and light of God. Fundamentalist Christians would be more severe with many being sent to hell. Some even believe that some people are predestined to be damned. The stress here is on the absolute holiness of God.
- **Heaven** – many hold non-literal ideas about heaven, taking the images in Scripture and artwork as symbolic. Catholics would agree. Heaven is eternal life in the presence of God.
- **Hell** – liberal Christians tend to think that a loving God would not allow anyone to be damned.

Now test yourself

TESTED

1 Give two ways the resurrection of Jesus has shaped what Christians believe about resurrection.
2 What idea of resurrection was St Paul trying to get across with his image of a seed?
3 Write down two Catholic beliefs about life after death.
4 Explain two different beliefs about (a) judgement and (b) hell that Christians have.

Sources of authority

Scripture: The Rich Man and Lazarus

The story of the Rich Man and Lazarus (Luke 16:19–31) reveals a great deal about Christian understandings of the Four Last Things, about Eschatology.

The parable is a story about particular judgement:
- The Rich Man is greedy and uncaring, ignoring the beggar called Lazarus at his gate.
- In death, the fortunes of the two men are reversed. The poor man is in the 'bosom of Abraham' (heaven) and the Rich Man in Hades (hell). There is a chasm between him and the poor man, as there was on earth between his riches and the man's poverty.
- The rich man calls out and asks to be shown mercy. Then he asks for someone to tell his brothers that if they live like he did that they will also be sent to hell. He thinks that if they were shown someone rising from the dead they would be convinced to change their ways.
- He is told that if they have not listened to Moses and the prophets, then nothing will convince them to change their attitudes.

Meaning and significance

God will judge us for all the actions we take in our lives when we die, including how we have treated others.

If we treat others well we will go to heaven, but if we don't follow the teachings of Jesus and prophets and treat others badly then we will go to hell. (Though some people believe that Hades in the story refers to purgatory rather than hell.)

Tradition: cosmic reconciliation

Revelations of Divine Love was the first book published by a woman in English.

Julian of Norwich (c. 1342–1416) received sixteen 'shewings' (showings) or 'revelations'. These came to her in 1373 at the time of the Black Death and great suffering in England and Europe. These revelations from God are essentially about the love of God and how this will have the final word in each life and in the world: all would be well.

Her 'shewings' have the idea of a cosmic reconciliation where all things will be drawn together in the love of God at the end of time. This was to be made possible because of the death of Christ on the cross for the redemption of the world.

Julian ended her days as Mother Julian, living in a prayer cell (room) in the walls of a church in Norwich.

> But Jesus, who in this vision informed me of all that is needed by me, answered with these words and said, 'It was necessary that there should be sin; but all shall be well, and all shall be well, and all manner of thing shall be well.' These words were said most tenderly showing no manner of blame to me nor any who shall be saved.'
> (Julian of Norwich, *Revelations of Divine Love*, 32)

Magisterium: Catholic understanding of eschatology

REVISED

Lumen gentium, a document from the Second Vatican Council, picks up on the idea of cosmic reconciliation or 'the restoration of all things'. This will happen at the end of time (or, to use Biblical language, 'the fullness of time'.)

> At that time the human race as well as the entire world, which is intimately related to man and attains to its end through him, will be perfectly re-established in Christ. (*Lumen gentium*, 48)

Lumen Gentium reminds people that Christ will return one day in glory:

> Since however we know not the day nor the hour, on Our Lord's advice we must be constantly vigilant. (*Lumen gentium*, 48)

The *Catechism of the Catholic Church* teaches that God does not wish for anyone to be in hell and to be lost. In the eucharistic liturgy, the mercy of God is asked for from God who does not want 'any to perish, but all come to repentance'.

> God predestines no one to go to hell; for this, a wilful turning away from God (a mortal sin) is necessary and persistence in it until at the end. (*Catechism of the Catholic Church*, 1037)

Now test yourself

TESTED

1 How does the story of the Rich Man and Lazarus show the idea of particular judgement?
2 Why do some scholars think that it is not hell where the Rich Man is?
3 Who was Julian of Norwich, what did she write, and what idea of final judgement did she teach?
4 Sum up the teaching of *Lumen gentium*, 48 in a sentence.
5 What does the *Catechism of the Catholic Church* say about souls and hell?

Practices – liturgies of life and death

The last rites

REVISED

Three sacraments are involved in the rites that are given when a person is in danger of dying. These are confession (penance or reconciliation), holy communion and the anointing of the sick (sometimes called extreme unction when given at the point of death).

- **Confession** – reconciliation with God and forgiveness of sins before they pass on.
- **Holy communion** – taking the eucharistic host, the body of Christ, as 'food for the journey' ('viaticum'). Eating the eucharistic host reminds the person that Christ is in them, securing their hope of eternal life.
- **Anointing** – holy oil is used to pray for healing and strength as they prepare to depart this life.

Thus these aspects of the **last rites** are an expression of reconciliation, healing and hope.

> **Last rites** are the sacraments of confession, holy communion and anointing before a person dies.

The funeral rite

REVISED

Great care is taken with the body of the deceased and great respect is shown when the funeral takes place.

- The body, when prepared, will be kept in the undertaker's chapel, or be taken into church the night before. This 'wake' allows prayers and condolences before the funeral.
- The funeral can have prayers and readings only or a mass, usually known as a funeral mass or a requiem mass. Then the mass is offered for the soul of the deceased.
- The coffin is sprinkled with holy water as a reminder of baptism and the hope of eternal life. Sometimes a white cloth, a pall, is placed over the coffin to recall this also as this is like the white garment placed upon the newly baptised person.
- Incense is used around the coffin to honour the deceased, to remember that the person was made in the image of God, and to symbolise prayers being offered, and, in a sense, the presence of God himself.
- The Prayer of Commendation ends the funeral rite when the saints and the angels are asked to guide the departed into the presence of God.
- The Committal offers the deceased back to God and their body to the earth, 'dust to dust, ashes to ashes.' This can be at the graveside or at the crematorium. Prayers are also offered for the mourners that 'every tear will be wiped away'.

The sanctity of life

REVISED

Catholics believe that life is a gift from God.

- Each human being is believed to be created in the image of God, having reason, morality and love within them.

- The respect and the image of God idea is known as the **sanctity of life**. This means a person belongs to God more than they do to themselves.

Care for the dying and euthanasia

People who are dying are often in physical or mental pain. Christians see that suffering is sometimes a fact of life and carers have to work with it and through it.

However, Catholics believe that they should take care of people who are dying, showing compassion and respect for life as a gift from God.

- Spiritual care of the dying is shown when priest administer the last rites and when lay visitors comfort them and take them holy communion.
- Palliative care means pain-relieving care. This is offered in special hospital wards or in a hospice. Hospices are specially set up to offer this end-of-life care. Many hospices were set up by Christian groups.

Sometimes people who are in a lot of pain may want to end their life before it ends naturally. **Euthanasia** is when someone helps someone to die to relieve their suffering. Euthanasia is illegal in the UK but political pressure is trying to change the law.

- Catholics are opposed to euthanasia as this does not let nature take its course and makes us responsible for when a person dies. If life is a gift from God, people should not take it. 'Assisted dying' is another term for this and while it can seem compassionate, much medication and palliative care can relieve much suffering and allow the dying time to say farewells and gradually depart when ready.
- Catholics believe that people should be supported and given appropriate care so they don't feel they need to end their lives.
- However, Catholics don't believe that people should be kept alive at all costs, when there is no hope of recovery. Catholics believe that treatment can be withdrawn so that a suffering person can die naturally. However, essentials such as fluids should not be stopped unless death is near and these have clearly ceased to be effective.

Sanctity of life is the belief that each individual is made in the image of God and their life is a gift from God.

Euthanasia means 'a good death', meaning that medical staff intervene to end a sick person's life before they die naturally.

> Everyone has the duty to lead his or her life in accordance with God's plan. That life is entrusted to the individual as a good that must bear fruit already here on earth, but finds its full perfection only in eternal life. (*Declaration on Euthanasia*, 1)
>
> Discontinuing medical procedures that are burdensome, dangerous, extraordinary, or disproportionate to the expected outcome can be legitimate; it is the refusal of 'overzealous treatment'. Here one does not wish to cause death; one's inability to impede it is merely accepted. (*Catechism of the Catholic Church*, 2278)

Now test yourself

TESTED ☐

1 What three actions are contained in the last rites?
2 Give two ways the last rites show Catholic beliefs about eschatology.
3 How do the last rites and aspects of the funeral service encourage hope?
4 Give two ways Catholic beliefs about eschatology are reflected in the funeral rite.
5 Explain two ways Catholic beliefs about the sanctity of life affect how they care for the dying.

Exam practice: Creation

1 Roman Catholics believe they have to look after the world. What is the term for this?
   A   Sanctity of life   B   Stewardship   C   Creation   D   Responsibility   [1]
3 In which book of the Bible is the creation story found?
   A   Genesis   B   Exodus   C   Leviticus   D   Deuteronomy   [1]
5 Give two ideas about God expressed in the statement 'God is omnipotent'.   [2]
6 Give two reasons why belief in natural law is important to Roman Catholics.   [2]
7 Give two characteristics of God.   [2]
8 Explain two contrasting Christian beliefs about how the duty of stewardship should be carried out.   [4]
9 Explain two ways in which belief in free will influences Catholics today.   [4]
10 Explain two similar Christian beliefs about the Bible.   [4]
11 Explain two ways in which art expresses beliefs about God as creator. Refer **to scripture or another source of Christian belief and teaching** in your answer.   [5]
12 Explain two Christian beliefs about the creation. Refer **to scripture or another source of Christian belief and teaching** in your answer.   [5]
13 Explain two ways in which belief in natural law influences Catholic views about the sanctity of life. Refer **to scripture or another source of Christian belief and teaching** in your answer.   [5]
14 'The Bible is the absolute word of God.' Evaluate this statement. In your answer you should:
   ● give developed arguments to support this statement
   ● give developed arguments to support a different point of view
   ● refer to Christian teaching
   ● reach a justified conclusion.   [12]
15 'For Catholics, there is no clash between science and religion.' Evaluate this statement. In your answer you should:
   ● give developed arguments to support this statement
   ● give developed arguments to support a different point of view
   ● refer to Christian teaching
   ● reach a justified conclusion.   [12]
16 'It is more important for Catholics to love their neighbour than for them to care about the environment.' Evaluate this statement. In your answer you should:
   ● give developed arguments to support this statement
   ● give developed arguments to support a different point of view
   ● refer to Christian teaching
   ● reach a justified conclusion.   [12]

ONLINE

Commentary

Grade 2 candidates have limited knowledge of the content of the course. They write very short answers, sometimes giving no answer at all. If this is you, get notes that you can revise from, and learn methods of revision so that you can tackle the exam more effectively.

Grade 5 candidates have general knowledge of the topics, but they don't go into detail often enough. Their answers can be very vague or woolly, or they can be great on one question and very poor on another – showing patchy knowledge and understanding. If this is you, make sure you have notes that make sense to you, that cover every bit of the specification, and practise by making yourself explain everything – which comes from understanding the content better.

Grade 8 candidates have a strong understanding of the whole specification content; their answers are detailed and clear, reflecting that good understanding. Their writing demonstrates that they understand the connections between the different elements they have studied so that they readily refer to other elements where relevant.

Exam practice: Incarnation

1 Which of these is NOT a symbol specifically for Jesus?
   A Cross   B Crucifix   C Chi-Rho   D Alpha and omega   [1]

2 Catholics believe in the Incarnation. What is this?
   A The death of Jesus   C Jesus as a human
   B God revealed as a human   D The Trinity   [1]

3 Give two ideas about Jesus found in St Mark's Gospel.   [2]

4 Give two reasons why Catholics follow the teachings of Jesus.   [2]

5 Give two examples of moral teachings given by Jesus.   [2]

6 Explain two contrasting Christian beliefs about the importance of the sacraments.   [4]

7 Explain two ways in which belief in the incarnation influences Catholic understandings of the relevance of God in their lives today.   [4]

8 Explain two Christian beliefs about the Jesus as the fulfilment of the Law.   [4]

9 Explain two ways in which Catholics are influenced by the concept of *imago dei* in terms of the protection of the unborn child. Refer to **scripture or another source of Christian belief and teaching** in your answer.   [5]

10 Explain two Christian beliefs about the importance of Jesus as Son of God. Refer to **scripture or another source of Christian belief and teaching** in your answer.   [5]

11 Explain two ways in which religious art expresses beliefs about the Incarnation. Refer to **scripture or another source of Christian belief and teaching** in your answer.   [5]

12 'Statues of Jesus are important to help believers to understand God.' Evaluate this statement. In your answer you should:
- give developed arguments to support this statement
- give developed arguments to support a different point of view
- refer to Christian teaching
- reach a justified conclusion.   [12]

13 'For Catholics, it is not important to keep all the sacraments.' Evaluate this statement. In your answer you should:
- give developed arguments to support this statement
- give developed arguments to support a different point of view
- refer to Christian teaching
- reach a justified conclusion.   [12]

14 'Jesus' teaching in the Parable of the Sheep and Goats (Matthew 25:31-46) is his most important teaching.' Evaluate this statement. In your answer you should:
- give developed arguments to support this statement
- give developed arguments to support a different point of view
- refer to Christian teaching
- reach a justified conclusion.   [12]

ONLINE

Commentary

Grade 2 candidates make little use of quotations and/or teachings – 'limited reference to sources of wisdom and authority'. When used, they are the most common, but often not the most appropriate for the question so the examiner is left trying to work out how they are relevant (they won't!). Those used are usually not applied to the question – they can just sit there, almost irrelevant! They hardly ever use specifically Catholic teachings. If this is you, get a stock of basic teachings for the religions you study, and practise using them.

Grade 5 candidates use some quotes/teachings, but they can usually be more appropriate or better applied to the question. They are generally accurate, but could be sharper. If this is you, then you need to do more work on learning these teachings and making better use of them.

Grade 8 candidates make 'well-integrated reference to sources of wisdom and authority', in other words – they use lots of quotes/teachings which are specific to the question, which come from outside the Specification, and which they explain well in relation to the question. It is clear they have a deep understanding of the religion, and this is evidence of that.

Exam practice: Triune God, mission and prayer

1 Which of the following is not a mass setting?
   A Lord's Prayer   B Gloria   C Alleluia   D Sanctus   [1]
2 How many persons are there in the Trinity?
   A 1   B 2   C 3   D 4   [1]
3 Give two persons of the Trinity.   [2]
4 Give two reasons why baptism is important to Catholics.   [2]
5 Give two forms of music used in Catholic worship.   [2]
6 Explain two contrasting Christian beliefs about the intimacy of God's love.   [4]
7 Explain two ways in which belief in the Trinity has influenced Catholic interpretations of
   the creation.   [4]
8 Explain two ways in which prayer influences Christian life today.   [4]
9 Explain two ways in which prayer expresses beliefs about God. Refer to **scripture or another
   source of Christian belief and teaching** in your answer.   [5]
10 Explain two Christian beliefs that the Nicene Creed helps us to understand about the Trinity.
   Refer to **scripture or another source of Christian belief and teaching** in your answer.   [5]
11 Explain two ways in which baptism acts as a sign of initiation and participation in the life of God
   for Catholics. Refer to **scripture or another source of Christian belief and teaching** in your
   answer.   [5]
12 'Baptism is the most important sacrament for Catholics.' Evaluate this statement. In your
   answer you should:
   ● give developed arguments to support this statement
   ● give developed arguments to support a different point of view
   ● refer to Christian teaching
   ● reach a justified conclusion.   [12]
13 'The Mass is the only act of worship a Catholic need attend.' Evaluate this statement. In your
   answer you should:
   ● give developed arguments to support this statement
   ● give developed arguments to support a different point of view
   ● refer to Christian teaching
   ● reach a justified conclusion.   [12]
14 'Formal prayer does not help 'raise the heart and mind to God'.' Evaluate this statement. In your
   answer you should:
   ● give developed arguments to support this statement
   ● give developed arguments to support a different point of view
   ● refer to Christian teaching
   ● reach a justified conclusion.   [12]

ONLINE

Commentary

Grade 2 candidates write in a very limited way. They often write only a few words or a single sentence – no matter how many marks a question is worth. They also miss out questions. If this is you, then part of the problem is having too little knowledge – get notes which work for you, learn revision techniques which work for you, and use them. You will then have more to say in the exam.

Grade 5 candidates write in sentences and paragraphs. They usually try to extend their writing in all their answers. However, they may write less fluently than higher grade candidates, and so the quality is less good. If this is you, you need to learn and understand the topics better – that gives you more to write from, and when we have confidence in our understanding, we write better and fuller answers.

Grade 8 candidates write fluently and in good, detailed English. Their work flows, using connectives and paragraphing well to give an impression of having good command of the subject.

Exam practice: Redemption

1 Which of the following represents the 'risen Christ'?
   A Lectern   B Crucifix   C Plain Cross   D Stations of the Cross   [1]
2 Which of these items is **not** a furnishing found in a church?
   A Lectern   B Altar   C Real Presence   D Font   [1]
3 Give two religious furnishings found in a church.   [2]
4 Give two teachings about redemption.   [2]
5 Give two reasons why the Eucharist is important to Catholics.   [2]
6 Explain two contrasting Christian beliefs about salvation.   [4]
7 Explain two ways in which belief in the story of redemption has influenced Catholic liturgy.   [4]
8 Explain two ways in which church architecture emphasises Catholic belief.   [4]
9 Explain two Christian beliefs about the Eucharist. Refer to **scripture or another source of Christian belief and teaching** in your answer.   [5]
10 Explain two Christian beliefs about Jesus' death as a 'restoration'. Refer to **scripture or another source of Christian belief and teaching** in your answer.   [5]
11 Explain two Christian beliefs about the conscience as the voice of God. Refer to **scripture or another source of Christian belief and teaching** in your answer.   [5]
12 'The Eucharist is only made special by the "real presence" of God.' Evaluate this statement. In your answer you should:
   ● give developed arguments to support this statement
   ● give developed arguments to support a different point of view
   ● refer to Christian teaching
   ● reach a justified conclusion.   [12]
13 'Redemption is the central message of Catholicism.' Evaluate this statement. In your answer you should:
   ● give developed arguments to support this statement
   ● give developed arguments to support a different point of view
   ● refer to Christian teaching
   ● reach a justified conclusion.   [12]
14 'For Catholics, the church is an essential space for worship.' Evaluate this statement. In your answer you should:
   ● give developed arguments to support this statement
   ● give developed arguments to support a different point of view
   ● refer to Christian teaching
   ● reach a justified conclusion.   [12]

ONLINE ☐

Commentary

Grade 2 candidates answer questions simply, and not always in the way asked. They mix up the 'command words' which are the key instructions of a question. They also fail to provide required information, especially the religious teachings. If this is you, you need to practise so that you are really clear on what the questions are asking. You also need to have a few teachings which you can use – don't bother learning them word for word as an approximation is usually good enough.

Grade 5 candidates do as the questions ask, but often not in enough detail, and also without providing enough teachings. This course demands them all the time – so you have to know some. If this is you, get a teacher to help you rewrite the teachings in a way that you can understand and learn, then learn them. Write reminders on the front of the exam paper before you start answering to help you as you do the exam.

Grade 8 candidates know and use a lot of teachings. This is part of how they demonstrate their very good subject knowledge and why they are worth the highest grades.

Exam practice: Church and Kingdom of God

1 Which of these is NOT one of the four marks of the Church?

   A Holy   B One   C Worldwide   D   Catholic   [1]

2 How many Stations of the Cross are there, traditionally?

   A 11   B 12   C 13   D   14   [1]

3 Give two reasons Mary is important in the Roman Catholic Church. [2]

4 Give two reasons why Catholics go on pilgrimages. [2]

5 Give two of the four key documents of the Second Vatican Council. [2]

6 Explain two ways in which pilgrimage influences Catholics today. [4]

7 Explain two ways in which believing in a religious vocation might influence Catholics today. [4]

8 Explain two Christian beliefs in the Kingdom of God might influence Catholics today. [4]

9 Explain two Christian beliefs about justice. Refer to **scripture or another source of Christian belief and teaching** in your answer. [5]

10 Explain two Christian beliefs about peace (as a sign of the Kingdom). Refer to **scripture or another source of Christian belief and teaching** in your answer. [5]

11 Explain two Christian beliefs about reconciliation. Refer to **scripture or another source of Christian belief and teaching** in your answer. [5]

12 'Every Roman Catholic should make a pilgrimage to Rome.' Evaluate this statement. In your answer you should:

- give developed arguments to support this statement
- give developed arguments to support a different point of view
- refer to Christian teaching
- reach a justified conclusion. [12]

13 'In today's world, the Magnificat is the first prayer a Catholic should say.' Evaluate this statement. In your answer you should:

- give developed arguments to support this statement
- give developed arguments to support a different point of view
- refer to Christian teaching
- reach a justified conclusion. [12]

14 'Catholic aid agencies (charities) should support all people in poverty.' Evaluate this statement. In your answer you should:

- give developed arguments to support this statement
- give developed arguments to support a different point of view
- refer to Christian teaching
- reach a justified conclusion. [12]

ONLINE ☐

Commentary

Grade 2 candidates usually only express opinions in the evaluation questions. They don't develop their reasoning, so answers can be a series of loose comments. If this is you, ask your teacher for examples of statements, and go through them to really understand the statements.

Grade 5 candidates can argue for and against statements. Their range of arguments may be limited, or the depth with which they argue them is limited. If this is you, is it depth or range? Practise by targeting whichever the weakness is.

Grade 8 candidates not only give a range of arguments to support different viewpoints, they also develop and explain those arguments to give good depth, and make convincing arguments.

Exam practice: Eschatology

1 When is the paschal candle first used?
   A Palm Sunday   C Holy Saturday
   B Good Friday   D Easter Sunday   [1]

2 Which of the following is not one of the 'last four things' at the end time?

   A Purgatory   B Judgement   C Heaven   D Hell   [1]
3 Give two symbols from the paschal candle.   [2]
4 Give two forms of memorial expression.   [2]
5 Give two beliefs about purgatory.   [2]
6 Explain two ways in which prayers are influenced by Catholic beliefs about life after death.   [4]
7 Explain two ways in which belief in the sanctity of life influences attitudes to euthanasia
   for Catholics today.   [4]
8 Explain two ways in which church belief in judgement influences Catholics today.   [4]
9 Explain two Christian beliefs about the end time. Refer to **scripture or another source of
   Christian belief and teaching** in your answer.   [5]
10 Explain two Christian beliefs about the last rites (i.e. the sacraments for the seriously ill or
   dying). Refer to **scripture or another source of Christian belief and teaching** in your answer.   [5]
11 Explain two Christian beliefs about the resurrection of Jesus. Refer to **scripture or another
   source of Christian belief and teaching** in your answer.   [5]
12 'It is not important to have memorials for the dead.' Evaluate this statement. In your answer you
   should:
   ● give developed arguments to support this statement
   ● give developed arguments to support a different point of view
   ● refer to Christian teaching
   ● reach a justified conclusion.   [12]
13 'The Parable of the Rich Man and Lazarus teaches Catholics to help the poor.' Evaluate this
   statement. In your answer you should:
   ● give developed arguments to support this statement
   ● give developed arguments to support a different point of view
   ● refer to Christian teaching
   ● reach a justified conclusion.   [12]
14 'Michelangelo's painting of the Last Judgement is a perfect representation of Catholic beliefs
   about life after death.' Evaluate this statement. In your answer you should:
   ● give developed arguments to support this statement
   ● give developed arguments to support a different point of view
   ● refer to Christian teaching
   ● reach a justified conclusion.   [12]

ONLINE ☐

Commentary

Grade 2 candidates have limited knowledge of the content of the course. They struggle to recognise key terms, and so find some questions difficult because they don't understand the central term. If this is you – learn key words to begin to help yourself.

Grade 5 candidates have general knowledge of the topics, so recognise most of the key terms. Their understanding of them may be limited, so they don't go into detail often enough. If this is you, practise by making yourself explain everything – which comes from understanding the content better.

Grade 8 candidates have a strong understanding of the content, and know the key terms well. They use more than just the obvious terms, and use them showing good understanding and application. Their answers are detailed and clear.

Judaism – beliefs and teachings

Key beliefs

The nature of God

REVISED

God as one and as creator

- The *Shema* (statement of belief) affirms belief in one God.
- Monotheism separated the Jews from others who were polytheists. Christians are also monotheists
- Belief in one God means belief in One Creator God who is indivisible and complete.
- God made the world *ex-nihilo* (from nothing) in his way and not dependent. The Jewish story of creation is found in the Book of Genesis describing the six days of creation and God resting on the seventh (hence the Shabbat day of rest). Christians also believe this.
- The world exists because God wills it to, he existed before anything else and is eternal and the world continues to exist because he wills it to.
- God revealed himself through his creation but remains incomprehensible.

The creation story, Genesis 1:1–2:3

God created the world in seven days, with the seventh being a day of rest.

Day 1 There was nothing, the earth was without form, just 'restless waters'. God created light, then called the darkness 'night' and the light 'day'. He saw it was good.

Day 2 God separated the firmament (heaven/sky) from the waters. It was good.

Day 3 God gathered the water to one place, revealing the lands. He created vegetation on the land. It was good.

Day 4 God put lights into the firmament – the sun, moon and stars – to divide day and night, and cause the seasons. The sun was light for the day, and the moon for the night. It was good.

Day 5 God created the fish of the sea and the birds of the air. He encouraged their reproduction – 'Be fruitful and multiply.' It was good.

Day 6 God created all living creatures on the land. And then humans in his image. God encouraged reproduction. God gave man power over all of creation. It was all good.

Day 7 God blessed the seventh day as holy.

God as lawgiver and judge

- Having created the world God wants humanity to live a certain way, for which they should follow his rules. If they do this, they will be serving God.
- God has given many laws (mitzvot); the first to Adam (not to eat from the tree) and the second to Noah after the flood.
- These laws (mitzvot) are a spiritual and ethical code of practice.
- God gave 613 laws which combine the Seven Laws of Noah, the Ten Commandments given to Moses and others. They cover all aspects of life both spiritual and material actions.
- The Tanakh also gives examples of people disobeying God's laws, and how God punished them.
- Jews believe that God will judge everyone resulting in punishment and reward.

Shekhinah – the divine presence

- This expresses how God is involved in the world. Humans cannot see God but people have said they have felt his presence.
- It has been described as a light created to connect God and the world or as 'the glory of God' surrounding people.
- Phrases such as 'the earth shone in his glory' or as 'a pillar of cloud by day and fire by night' or 'clouds covering something to be filled with God's presence' or reference to' God dwelling' in places all refer to this idea of Shekhinah.

How the nature of God influences Jewish people

- Jews believe that following the law is to please and serve God.
- All aspects of their lives are ruled by God including: family, food, clothing, business, interaction with others, worship and so on.
- Religious clothing like the tallith (prayer shawl) is a constant reminder of God's laws.
- God has, and will punish people for not following his laws.

Exam tip

Learn some historical examples of who has been punished by God and how so you can refer to them in your answers.

Exam tip

Revise the Seven Laws of Noah, the Ten Commandments and some examples of the kinds of things the 613 laws apply to in daily life. This gives you examples to use in answers, as well as helping you understand Judaism better.

Exam tip

Learn some of these phrases so you can refer to them showing how the scriptures describe how God is present in the world today.

Now test yourself

TESTED

1 What is the Shema?
2 Give two names for God.
3 Outline the Genesis creation story
4 What are mitzvot? Give examples of sets of mitzvot.
5 What is the Shekhinah?
6 How does belief in what God is like influence Jewish people in their lives?

Life after death

This is a very difficult topic in Jewish belief as it is clear we know nothing about death and we cannot explain rationally what will happen after death. Life after death is not a central belief for Jews and there are many views held, but what they do agree upon is that they do believe that this life is not the end of everything.

So what do Jewish holy books say?

- The Torah says nothing about an afterlife. It focuses more on this life now **(Olam Ha-Ze)**.
- There are references to the righteous being reunited with loved ones and that the not-so righteous will not be reunited with them.
- The Torah focuses more on this life now and repairing this world rather than on a life after death.
- Later prophets such as Daniel discuss the afterlife in terms of the body being created from dust (so will decay) but the soul comes from the presence of God (so will live on).

Resurrection

- The **resurrection** of the dead is a key belief, though not discussed in the Torah.
- Masorti Jews believe in resurrection but say our understanding is too limited to know clear details. Reform Jews believe this too but 'this life now' is more important.
- Efforts to repair the world are a way to a good afterlife.
- Resurrection will happen in the Messianic Age – the righteous dead will rise and evil people will not be resurrected.

Reincarnation

- Some believe this is happening all the time – souls are reborn to continue *tikkun olam* (repairing the world) so this should be their focus.
- **Reincarnation** allows the soul to fulfil the mitzvot showing a compassionate God giving the soul a second chance to get it right.

Olam Ha-Ze is life in the present, here and now.

Resurrection is a physical coming back of the body to life after death.

Reincarnation is the rebirth of the soul.

Olam Ha-Ba is the world that is to come.

Gan Eden is a place good people go when they die.

Gehenna is a place associated with hell.

What life after death might look like

The world to come – Olam Ha-Ba

- This is like a perfect version of the world that will exist at the end of days after the Messiah has come and God has judged the living and the dead.
- The righteous will rise to **Olam Ha-Ba** (not described in scripture, but thought of as a spiritual realm where souls go at death). Jews must therefore act wisely.
- Olam Ha-Ba has to be prepared for by doing good deeds and knowing the Torah (like the perfect Shabbat) – hence Jews strive to be good people now, and to repair the world.
- This can be seen in two ways; first as life after the Messiah, or second as a place where souls go at death or in the future.

Gan Eden

- There is no clear picture as to what this is and how it fits in the afterlife.
- Some say it's a good place people go when they die (but at what point after death that is, is unclear).
- All nations sit and eat in **Gan Eden** when the peaceful Messianic Age comes.

Gehenna

- Associated with hell, but more a place of cleansing of the soul for less than 12 months – then they move to Olam Ha-Ba.
- **Gehenna** is a place to see and be remorseful for wrongdoings, not eternal punishment.
- Some Jews think the soul of an evil person ceases to exist after 12 months whereas others believe the soul remains in a state of remorse.
- Anyone who does not live by the Torah will spend time there.

Overall, the idea of the afterlife is incomprehensible. Jews emphasise the need to focus on this life, as if they do good here and now, then what happens in the afterlife takes care of itself.

Now test yourself

1 What is the difference between resurrection and reincarnation in Judaism?
2 What are Olam Ha-Ze, and Olam Ha-Ba?
3 Describe Gan Eden and Gehenna.
4 Why do most Jews believe it is more important to focus on this life not the next?

Influences

I am not sure what will happen after death, so I live now as if something will! I worship God my creator, I treat others with respect and kindness, I live by the commandments. It is important to be a good person, but also to show devotion to God.

The Messiah

What does 'messiah' mean?

- It is not God as he will be born of human parents.
- The Hebrew *moshiach* means anointed one.
- He will be a descendent of King David (second king of Israel).
- The term is used in the books of the Torah.

How will the Age of the Messiah happen?

- It will be announced by the Prophet Elijah.
- Graves will open and the dead will rise.
- A human figure will be sent by God to bring in a new era of peace – the Messianic Age.

When will this happen?

- Some Jewish scholars believe God has set aside a specific date, so when God decides, really.
- Others say the conduct of society has to improve before a Messianic Age can happen.
- There are two options: first, when humans deserve it the most, because their beliefs and behaviour are better, or second, when life is so terrible that humans need it the most.

What are Jews told the messiah will be like?

- He will be a great political leader descended from King David who fully understands and keeps Jewish law.
- He will be a charismatic leader who inspires people to follow him.
- He will be a military leader and a righteous judge, but not a god or supernatural.

What will the messiah do?

- He will bring political and spiritual peace to Israel, and Jerusalem will be restored.
- A government will be set up in Jerusalem for all the peoples of the world.
- He will rebuild the Temple and set up worship as it should be.
- Jewish law and the religious court system will be re-established as the law everywhere.

What will the Messianic Age be like?

- People will live together in peace with no hatred or intolerance or sin.
- Animals will no longer prey on each other and crops will be plentiful.
- All Jews will return to Israel and all people will recognise the Jewish God as the true God.
- All people will understand religious truths so religion will no longer divide people.
- Note – it is a bit like what Christians generally believe heaven to be like!

Influences

The Messiah's coming depends on us – so I keep the mitzvot, and try to do my bit for making the world a better place. I live in hope that I will see the Messiah in my lifetime.

Now test yourself

1 What is the Messiah?
2 What is the Messianic Age?
3 How and when will the Messianic Age happen?
4 What will the Messiah do?

The covenant and the mitzvot

Covenants

REVISED ☐

For this course you need to know about the covenants with Abraham and Moses.

A covenant (*berith*) creates a permanent link between the past, present and future that will never be dissolved. God needed a people to 'dwell' in, who would serve him and prepare the world for a future time when all humans would know God. If the Jews did this God would never abandon them.

> A **covenant** is an agreement between God and mankind.

The chosen people of God

- Out of all of earth's people the Lord chose the Jews as his treasured possession.
- The idea of being chosen brings with it responsibility.
- The job is to serve God through the laws, rather than gaining privilege from having been chosen.
- Jews believe others have responsibilities to God too – just a different one to theirs.
- They will always be the chosen people – an everlasting covenant.
- Jews believe the offer was made to all peoples but only taken up by the Jews.

The covenant with Abraham Abram)

REVISED ☐

Who was he?

- His father believed in many gods but Abram believe the world was created by one God.
- He was told by God to go to the promised land where he would make a great nation and be the father of it.
- He was married to a woman named Sarai and because they had no children he took another wife (who bore a son), but then Sarai bore a son too, called Isaac (meaning 'laughter'). Abram was renamed Abraham (father of many). Sarai became Sarah (princess).

About the covenant

- God promised Abraham land and descendants (hence he is seen as the Father of the Jewish nation).
- Abraham would only ever worship one God and be obedient to him.
- The symbol was the circumcision of male babies.

The impact of Abraham – why is he so important?

- This first covenant connected the Jews to God before the Torah was written.
- Abraham had his faith in God tested 10 times (the last being the sacrifice of his son Isaac).
- Both he and Isaac passed the test, so God knew Isaac would carry on his father's work.
- Abraham was the founding father of Judaism, and the circumcision of all males unites the children of Israel.
- For God this begins the idea of the 'promised land' so giving the Jewish nation a homeland.
- For Jews, Abraham is a role model of belief in and worship of their one God.

The covenant with Moses

REVISED

Who was he?

- Born into slavery in Egypt, Moses was saved from the Pharaoh's order to kill all Israelite babies by being placed by his mother in a reed basket in the river. He was found by an Egyptian princess who brought him up.
- Later he had to flee Egypt after he attacked an Egyptian guard who had attacked an Israelite slave.
- Moses was ordered by God to set the Israelite people free, and with God's help via the sending of the Ten Plagues they were released.
- He was given the Ten Commandments and the Torah by God and led to the Promised Land.

About the covenant

- Moses was given the Laws as well as their interpretation.
- His people promised to follow the Laws (Ten Commandments and mitzvot).
- God would continue to give the people his blessings as his chosen people.
- The sabbath day of rest was the physical symbol.

The impact of Moses – why is he so important?)

- He freed the Israelite people from slavery.
- He led the chosen people to the promised land so they were no longer a nomadic people.
- He laid down the laws that bind all Jews to God and so by their observance Jews continue to serve God.

Influences

If I believe God set up covenants with my people, then I have to keep to my side of that agreement; following the mitzvot does that. I also feel I have good role models in Abraham and Moses, so can look to their tenacity, humbleness and devotion to God and try to also be like that.

Now the Lord said to Abram, 'Go from your country and your kindred and your father's house to the land that I will show you. And I will make of you a great nation, and I will bless you, and make your name great, so that you will be a blessing. (Genesis, 12:1–3)

Now test yourself

TESTED

1 What is a covenant?
2 Who was Abraham and why was he important?
3 What were the two sides of the covenant between God and Abraham?
4 Who was Moses?
5 Why is Moses an important role model for Jews?
6 What was the covenant between Moses and God?

Commentaries on Exam Practice answers at **www.hoddereducation.co.uk/myrevisionnotes**

Laws (mitzvot) and reasons for observance

- The mitzvot are the 613 laws given to Moses.
- They are the rules of God found in the Torah.
- They govern every aspect of Jewish life – covering rituals of worship and ethics to do with morality.
- Jews agree to follow them as part of the covenants.
- Some laws are judgements such as 'thou shall not kill'. These are called *mishpatim*.
- Some are statutes (*chukim*), that is, laws testing faith. The reasons for these laws and this type of law are only known to God.
- These laws bind the Jewish nation; the well-being of the nation depends on keeping these laws.
- Observance of the laws separates Jews from non-Jews, making them a distinct group.

The Ten Commandments

- They are found in Exodus 20:1–17, and repeated in Deuteronomy 5:6–21.
- These ten laws are found in the Torah and are directed at people forever. They are a condensed version of the 613 mitzvot written on tablets of stone by God for Moses.
- They are essential to Jewish life to serve God, and together with the Torah they form the sources of authority for Jewish life.
- They are depicted over the ark in the synagogue, and are a standard feature of all synagogues quite often depicted additionally elsewhere, for example, in stained-glass windows, and on the outside of synagogues.
- Following the Ten Commandments builds society, as it sets a baseline of moral behaviour. If everyone followed these Ten Commandments, society would be one of harmony and respect from, to and by all.
- Four of the Ten Laws are about God (e.g. Keep the Sabbath holy.) and six concern our relationships with each other (e.g. Do not bear false witness.).

613 mitzvot

- 356 of the 613 are commands to 'not do' and 248 are commands 'to do'.
- They are listed in the Mishnah Torah written by Maimonides.
- These laws are religious laws encompassing all aspects of daily life that are intended to build a better person and more harmonious society.
- The mitzvot cover areas such as food, business practices, punishments, agriculture, clothing, wars, the poor, God, rituals, the Temple and many more.

Influences

If I believe God has given these laws, then I should follow them.
By following the laws, I 'walk the right path' and will be rewarded.
These laws give structure and security to my actions, which I find comforting.

Mitzvot between humans and God

REVISED

- The mitzvot show God reaching out to his people and vice versa.
- Jews believe God also gave Moses the *halakha* (an interpretation of the laws).
- The *halakha* is 'the path that one walks' and by following the laws Jews are doing as God wants. It is added to by rabbis to keep Jewish life up to date in the modern world.

- There are six constant mitzvot – to know there is a God, to not believe in other gods, that God is one, to love God, to fear God and not to be misled by your heart or eyes.
- Jews are encouraged not just to believe in God but also to know him (by study) in mind and to love him (in their hearts).
- All mitzvot bring Jewish people 'closer' to God and so they underpin the whole of Judaism.

Mitzvot between human and human

REVISED

- These relate to action towards others – family and neighbours – creating a code of ethics.
- Each law is also a guiding principle.
- If Jews act in a responsible way, God is pleased, His goodness flows through people so God and

humans are closer. This means the act of serving God is fulfilled.
- Following the law is 'walking in the path', fulfilling their part of the covenant and bringing God's holiness to the world ready for the time when all humans will know God.

Free will and the 613 mitzvot

REVISED

- Free will is having the ability to make decisions, and to choose right from wrong.
- Without free will, actions have no religious or moral value.
- In the Torah God has a role in determining what humans do but it is also clear that humans choose what to do.
- Rewards and punishments follow choices. The 613 mitzvot tell Jews how to do good, and avoid evil, since humans have the power to do either.
- Sometimes humans cannot control what happens, but they can control their reaction to it, such as responding to suffering by showing compassion or helping, responding to persecution by standing up against it, being strong rather than giving up in the face of difficulty and so on.

Free will – how do Jews know humans have it?

- Genesis says that humans know good from evil.
- However, knowing good is not a guarantee that humans will do good; punishment follows evil acts. If a person can be punished, by definition, they have had free will to be able to do the punishable act.
- Orthodox Jews follow the mitzvot strictly, so their free will is directed to obeying; Reform Jews say some are open to interpretation, so they use their free will to decide whether to obey.

Now test yourself

TESTED

1 What are mitzvot?
2 What are *mishpatim*?
3 Where would you find the Ten Commandments?
4 Explain the difference between mitzvot between God and human, and between human and human.
5 What is free will?

Key moral principles

Tikkun olam – healing the world

Mankind has a responsibility to heal or restore and change the world.

- On a fundamental level, they do it through keeping Shabbat. This is a day when Jews renew their efforts to bring about a better world.
- Found in the Mishnah (the first writings of the oral laws by rabbis) – *tikkun olam* teaches doing actions not because holy texts say so, but rather because it helps create social harmony.
- Ethical mitzvot – to be a Jew is to live and work as a collective to create a better world. If these laws are followed then the world will be repaired.
- The more people do this, the more the world is repaired and nearer it is to the Messianic Age.
- Prayer – the Aleinu prayer (said three times a day) implies that Jews should heal the world so that the goodness of God can shine through.
- Many Jews pray for the harmony of nations, the uniting of people, no more hatred, where the sick are healed and the damage done by humans to humans' ends.
- Through this desire to heal the world Jews hope that their actions will be an inspiration to others to follow suit, whether they are religious or not.
- Orthodox Jews believe *tikkun olam* comes from following the Mitzvot; Reform Jews believe it needs to be done in a practical way.

> *Tikkun olam* is the Hebrew word meaning to repair or heal the world.
>
> *Tzedakah* is charity and giving to the poor bonding together with justice.

Justice and charity

Micah says God requires them to 'only do justice, love kindness and walk humbly with God.'

- Jews believe their wealth is on loan from God. By helping the less fortunate through the means of charity, this brings justice to the poor.
- Hence, *tzedakah* is as much about justice as it is about charity.
- Jewish believe that giving *tzedakah* has the power to change the world. This is because when you help people they become more able and empowered, and the injustice they are subject to is made a little less.
- Jews support many areas that promote justice, including social justice for different races, sexes, disabilities and sexualities. They work for religious freedoms, women's rights, the rights of people to live in a safe world, for example, helping street children in poverty or the need for stronger American gun laws.

Exam tip

Make sure you know the work of Tzedek as this will give you some practical examples of how Jews work for justice through charity.

Loving kindness – what does *chesed* mean and what does it involve?

'The world is built on **chesed**.' (Psalm 89:3)

- This virtue also contributes to *tikkun olam*, because out of kindness we try to heal the world.
- It is central to the Commandments as it focuses on peoples' relationships with each other.
- Jews believe that God's creation was a clear act of *chesed* and he sustains the world through *chesed*.
- The Pirkei Avot states the world stands on the Torah, service of God and acts of *chesed*.
- The world will always be difficult but *chesed* can make many situations better.
- It is the loving intention behind these acts, rather than just doing these acts that is important.
- *Chesed* is about personal service, personal attitudes and efforts of the heart and includes all aspects of life – people, animals and the environment.
- *Chesed* can be done for rich and poor, the living and the dead and with money and actions.
- No one should harm another, or take advantage of others' misfortune. This would be the opposite of *chesed*.

> **Chesed** is the Hebrew word for loving kindness.

Influences

I believe that *tzedakah* is a really important attitude to have. It isn't just about charity; believing in justice means I want to help because by giving charity means I restore some element of justice. This world, which God created needs to be looked after – *tikkun olam* – so I try to live in a way which contributes to looking after it. I also try to practice *chesed* in my life every day. It doesn't hurt or cost anything to be kind to others, but helps them and I feel good – so why not!

Now test yourself

TESTED ☐

1 What do we mean by 'moral principles'?
2 What is *tikkun olam*? Give examples.
3 What is *tzedek*? Give examples.
4 What is *chesed*?
5 How might a Jewish person show *chesed*?
6 Why are the three moral principles (*tikkun olam*, *tzedakah*, *chesed*) so important?

Pikuach nefesh

This is the belief that the saving or preservation of human life takes precedence over everything because 'life is sacred.'

The sanctity of human life

- God made humans special; he breathed life into them, gave them free will and gave them a soul.
- The human task was to carry out *tikkun olam* and to work for a close relationship with God.
- The human soul is made in the image of God.
- Life is sacred even beyond the law so rules can be broken to save it – even Shabbat rules!
- Each Jewish person has a purpose – to live as God wants through the Torah and mitzvot. Their aim is to change and repair the world from evil and horror to peace and harmony. They have a duty to make the most of the gift of life.
- No human can take life – unless in self-defence, state punishment or in war.

So how does *pikuach nefesh* work?

In the Talmud there is the idea that people 'live' by the law – it protects life and helps them survive. So where laws may cause harm, (for example, by a doctor not helping someone because the Shabbat laws do not allow him to work) the law must be set aside because 'saving life' is more important.

- Jews are required to break the law in cases where life is at risk – animal or human.
- If it is unclear whether life is actually at risk then action should be taken as if it is in danger – waiting might cause more harm.
- It also applies to occasions where life shortening issues happen – organ donation is allowed to continue the life of the patient (as long as the giver's life is not at risk).
- Autopsics can also be done if what is learnt helps saves lives in the future.
- In the world today Jews are involved in *pikuach nefesh* – as health workers, aid workers, environmental campaigners, police and fire services and peacekeeping soldiers, for example.

> **Exam tip**
>
> It is not always easy to apply this law though in the modern world. For your exam you can use these beliefs in topics about life and death, but you have to balance them out with the idea that sometimes taking life can prevent far more suffering long term. Use ideas from the four ethical themes you have studied here. It will show you have the ability to apply connections and show how beliefs affect decisions people make.

> **Revision tip**
>
> Try using mind-mapping diagrams as a way to remember all the topics. Look at the simple one below started for you covering all the Judaism beliefs topics. As the diagram becomes wider more information is added. The law section is started for you. Try your own as all our minds work differently – use the words and colours that will help you the most.

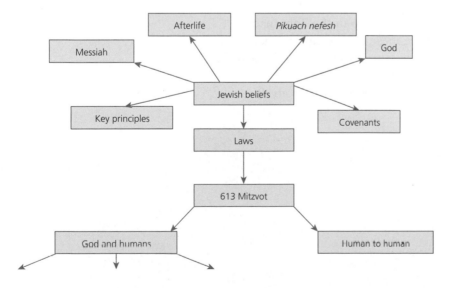

> ## Now test yourself
>
> 1 What does *pikuach nefesh* mean?
> 2 Explain the Jewish concept of sanctity of life.
> 3 How does *pikuach nefesh* impact on daily life for Jews?
>
> TESTED

Judaism – practices

The synagogue and worship

The synagogue and its importance

- A special place to worship God, to study the word of God (hence also called *shul*).
- Jews have always had a 'special place' to worship: Moses built a Tabernacle, Solomon built a Temple. The last temple was destroyed in Jerusalem in 70 CE. Away from Jerusalem, Jews worship in synagogues – representative of that one Temple.
- Synagogue means 'bringing together' emphasising community worship of God.
- It is a house of worship – a place for specific prayers to be said. A *minyan* (ten members) must be present for worship to take place.
- Has a community use and links the faith now to Jewish history and traditions.

Key features

Outside

The star of David (five-pointed star) symbol and the menorah (seven branched candlestick).

Inside

- **Aron hakodesh** – ark of the covenant housing the Torah and other scrolls. Represents the Holy of Holies, the most sacred part of the Temple and before it the Tabernacle. A cupboard in the eastern wall facing Jerusalem covered by a curtain (*parokhet*) to safeguard and glorify its contents. Lions of Judah holding the Ten Commandments are above it.
- **Ner tamid** – represents the ever-burning lamp in the Tabernacle showing the Torah should always have meaning – a light in the world's darkness. Traditionally an oil lamp it is seen as a symbol of Israel as the 'light of nations'.
- **Bimah** – raised platform where the Sefer Torah is read from. It represents the

Other elements in the synagogue

Dress

- Orthodox males wearing kippah, tallit and tefillin; whereas Reform Jews usually just kippah.

People

- The rabbi is the spiritual leader – a learned man of scripture and law who has attended Yeshivah – Reform allows women to hold this role too.
- The cantor sings prayers and often leads worship.

> **Some differences**
>
> - Orthodox use the name *'shul'*, Reform use 'temple' and Masorti use 'synagogue'.
> - Seating: Orthodox – women sit separately, all face the Bimah which is central to the room; Reform – all sit together, all face the Ark and Bimah at the front of the room.

Public acts of worship

REVISED

It is important to worship as:
- it forms part of the covenant, is a mitzvot and so a duty
- it keeps people mindful of God and shows their devotion
- it shows God worship and praise
- it brings the community together.

Structure

- Centred around different prayers from the *siddur* (prayer book) and *chamash* (printed Torah).
- Key prayers are the Shema, the Amidah, the Kaddish and Aleinu.
- On Shabbat, both Torah and prophecies will be read.

Worship is important both in the synagogue and in the home

- Synagogue worship includes – Shabbat services, daily services, festivals, rites of passage, study, holocaust memorials and so on.
- Worship at home includes Shabbat meals and prayers, study, circumcisions, variety of prayer and thanksgivings, and so on.

Now test yourself

TESTED

1 What is the place of worship for a Jew called?
2 Why is a communal place needed for worship?
3 What kinds of worship might be found in the home only, and in the synagogue only?
4 Why is worship important?

Prulyer

Hebrew word for prayer is **tefillah** – a time for reflection on their relationship with God and each other and on how they are following their duties.

Shema

- 'Hear, O Israel, the lord your God is one God.' Must be recited three times daily.
- Three sections follow the statement: one about God and religious duties, second about accepting and keeping the law and then to keep the mitzvot to wear tzitzit. Reform Jeux say only the first.

Amidah

- It is said while standing facing Jerusalem.
- 19 blessings: three for praise, thirteen requests and three thanksgivings.
- Spoken with the movement of lips rather than out loud – the sound comes from the heart.

Kaddish – holy

- A hymn of praise to God. There are different Kaddishes for different occasions.
- It can only be recited if there is a minyan; said each prayer time each day in the synagogue. It begins, 'May his great name be exalted ...'

Aleinu – praise and dedication

- It is said at the end of services.
- It reminds them that God's rule is eternal.
- It reminds them they are the chosen people and that that choosing brings with it difficulties.

Clothing for prayer

Prayer is done at home as well as in the synagogue. At home prayers are more personal and do not require a minyan. People must be in the right mindset (*kavanah*) and dressed in a respectful way for God.

Prayers are found in the **Siddur** having been shaped over the centuries by rabbinical teachings, and *minhagim* (traditions).

Kippah yarmulke

- Skullcap worn by Jewish men, as a sign of respect for God.

Tallit

- A prayer shawl worn around the shoulders.
- It has four corners for the four corners of the world. Each corner has tzitzit – fringes tied with five knots in them (five plus five on each side representing the Ten Commandments).
- The fringes hang loose to represent the 613 mitzvot. All are reminders of God's law being all around them and not to be forgotten.

Tefillin

- These are two small leather boxes with straps – one tied to the forehead and one on the arm. Each contains a passage of scripture.
- As the straps are put on, prayers are said to focus the mind.
- Jews pray at three set times: **Shacharit**, **Minchah**, and **Maariv**.
- Prayer is important to Jews because it's a mitzvot, shows devotion, sets people up for the day in the right way, links Jews to their history, it is a cleansing act and a channel of communication with God.

Shacharit is the morning prayer as Abraham did.

Minchah is the afternoon prayer following Isaac's timing of prayer.

Maariv is the evening prayer following Jacob's timing.

Now test yourself

TESTED

1 Name three prayers in Judaism
2 How many times a day should Jews pray? When are these?
3 How should a Jew prepare to pray?
4 Why is prayer important?

Shabbat

- Shabbat is the Jewish day of rest, beginning at sundown of Friday and ending on Saturday evening.
- It is a commandment to keep it holy.
- It is part of the Jewish covenant with God.
- It is reminder that God created the world and copying God's example of resting from work.
- The Talmud forbids 39 areas of work on Shabbat, covering *melachah* tasks (those which are creative or change one's environment).
- Remember – the principle of Pikuach Nefesh overrides Shabbat rules for work.

What is the order of Shabbat?

Getting ready

- The house is tidied, food is already made and the table set.
- Arrangements have to be made to ensure no work needs to be done.

Shabbat begins

- No later than 18 minutes before sunset, and before the meal two candles are lit. The mother passes her hands over her eyes and recites the blessing to welcome Shabbat.
- Two candles *zakhor* and *shamor* – *remember* and *observe* Shabbat.
- The family attends synagogue (only the men in Orthodox and Masorti traditions) and Shabbat prayers are said (Kabbalat – six chapters from Psalms, then maariv prayer, and seven Amidah blessings – 12 petitions are omitted as Shabbat provides for all).
- They return for a family meal – the children are blessed, Kiddush recited and prayers said over the wine to make Shabbat holy. The bread (challah) is blessed, songs are sung. It ends with a blessing.

On the Saturday

- The whole family attends the synagogue after the rituals of Kiddush and the two challah have been repeated.
- The reading of the Torah is central to this service after it has been paraded around the synagogue from the Ark to the Bimah.
- The message of the Torah portion is the theme of the sermon.

- The service is from the Siddur so everyone can follow it.
- Kiddush is shared at the end of the service – usually wine and cake.
- Orthodox Jews may spend the day in study of the Torah; for others it is family time; some use the day to do good deeds.
- Shabbat ends with the Havdalah-blessings recited over wine, candles and spices. Lighting candles is an act of work so indicates the separation of the Shabbat from other days.

What is the importance of Shabbat?

- It is a sacred time for all the family.
- It is a day of rest, separating this day from the other six in the week – a day to be 'right with God'.
- Religion is the focus of the day – it is a time to study and reflect.
- It brings the family and community together.
- It shows respect, devotion and duty to God.
- It shows all Jews are bound by the covenant promises, and honours tradition (*minhag*).

Now test yourself

1 Describe what happens at Shabbat.
2 Explain two ways that Shabbat is important for Jews today.
3 Explain why in Judaism it is necessary to have this separate day.
4 Explain the influence Shabbat celebration has on the lives of Jews.

TESTED

Tenakh

- The name for the full set of Holy scriptures of Judaism.
- The Law, Prophets and the Writings.

> The **Torah** is the Law consisting of five Books
>
> **Nevi'im** are the books of the Prophets.
>
> **Ketuvim** is the books of Writings.
>
> **Talmud** is the written interpretation of all Jewish civil and religious laws.
>
> **Mishnah** is a study of Jewish law.
>
> **Gemara** is a commentary on the Mishnah.
>
> **Midrash** is 'storytelling' – written by rabbis to interpret the Tenakh, or answer questions arising from it.

The Torah

- It is the religious law of Judaism.
- It has divine origins, it was given by God to Moses on Mt Sinai.
- The Torah links God and humanity.
- The mitzvot 'separate' Jews from others as they are part of the Covenant.
- It contains two types of laws – *mishpatim* (judgements) and *chukim* (statutes).
- The Torah is absolute (never-changing) and eternal (forever valid).

- During a year, in the synagogue the whole Torah will be read in 54 portions.
- Study of the Torah is essential and many Orthodox Jews devote their lives to this.
- Purpose for today: Torah means guidance or instruction – by following its rules Jews stay close to God.

The Nevi'im

- Are books containing the stories and teachings of the Prophets.
- Prophets are chosen by God to guide people and warn them about their behaviour.
- It's purpose for today: They provide the historical story of early Judaism, religious interpretations of the events and revelations from God. They also allow people to see the character of God by reading the stories.

The Ketuvim

- The 'writings' – it is unconnected books.
- It contain poetry, historical stories, songs and philosophical debates.
- Five of the books are used at five festivals –Pesach (Song of Songs), Shavuot (Ruth), Tishah B'Av (Lamentations), Sukkot (Ecclesiastes) and Purim (Esther).
- Its purpose for today: The underlying theme shows people commitment to God though endless difficulties and hard work.

Talmud – importance

- The Torah is timeless but difficult to apply throughout time.
- The Talmud relates today's problems to Torah law, interpreting the Laws so they are more easily understood and followed.
- Talmud means 'study' – greater study brings greater understanding allowing Jews to follow the laws better. It has been called an endless conversation through time about the law.

What does it look like? How does it work?

- The Talmud has in it the **Mishnah** (a study of the law) and the **Gemara** (a commentary on the Mishnah).
- The Mishnah sits in the centre of each page, flanked by sections of commentaries to help understanding.

- There are also Torah references so the reader can see what the study is about.
- The variety of commentaries and references show how Jewish thought and understanding has developed through time.

The Talmud keeps Jewish law and understanding up to date and applied to modern issues. Hence the Jewish Torah is always applicable and relevant.

Now test yourself

1 What makes up the Tenakh?
2 How does the Talmud differ from the Tenakh?
3 Why is the Talmud important to Jews, and how do they show this importance?

TESTED

Commentaries on Exam Practice answers at **www.hoddereducation.co.uk/myrevisionnotes**

Family life and festivals

Rituals and their significance

Certain stages in life are marked by Jews with a special celebration. They all have religion at the centre of those celebrations. They unite the religion in its past, present and future. For many of these there are significant differences between the rituals carried out by different types of Jews.

Birth ceremonies

For boys: brit malah

- Happens eight days after birth at home or in *shul* as soon as morning prayer ends.
- The boy is circumcised as a sign of the covenant and the way in which he becomes part of the Jewish faith.
- A **kvater** (godparent) takes the boy from his mother, and gives him to his father who wears his tallit and tefillin as a symbol of the commandments.
- The boy is then given to a **sandek** (special male) who holds the baby while the circumcision is done by the mohel.
- Candles are lit to remember when the idea of the room being lit up when Moses was born.
- The mohel blesses the baby, the father reads a passage from the Torah and then on completion of the circumcision the boy's name is announced.
- The boy is then fed by his mother and a celebratory meal is enjoyed.

For girls: zavid habit

- The tradition in some communities of welcoming girls.
- It is customary to name the girl in the synagogue after the father has been called to the Torah on the first Shabbat after her birth.
- The congregation sings to welcome her; the family provide **Kiddush** in celebration.
- Reform Jews take the girl to Shabbat services but in other communities she stays at home where a rabbi will come to bless her.

> **Brit milah** is the birth ceremony for a boy in Judaism.
>
> **Mohel** is a man trained to carry out circumcision.
>
> **Kvater** is a godparent to the baby.
>
> **Sandek** is a male person, specially chosen to hold the boy in the brit milah ceremony
>
> **Kiddush** is a blessing or ritual using wine.

Coming of age ceremonies

Bar mitzvah

- It means 'son of the commandment' and recognises that the boy has reached the age by which he is religiously responsible – a 'coming of age'.
- The boy reads the Torah in the synagogue on the Shabbat after his 13th birthday.
- He is now regarded as an adult – using tefillin in prayer and can be counted in a minyan. His father will say a public thank you that he no longer has the responsibility for his son's religious development.
- Many Jewish boys now go to Jerusalem for their bar mitzvah, making their Torah reading before the Western Wall (of the Temple).

Bat mitzvah

- It usually takes place at 12 years of age; means 'daughter of the commandment'.

- For Orthodox Jews it takes place at home with the girl reciting a blessing.
- For Reform Jews the girl may read from the Torah in the synagogue.

These ceremonies are important because the child consciously steps into the responsibility of being one with God's chosen people and confirms their wish to carry on in the religion. They also reinforce the togetherness of the community through great celebrations.

Now test yourself

1 What is brit milah?
2 What are bar and bat mitzvah?
3 What happens at a bar mitzvah?
4 Why are ceremonies of commitment important in Judaism?

Marriage

- Marriage is the most elaborate ceremony – it is full of custom and tradition.
- It fulfils the commandment in Genesis to 'Be fruitful and multiply.'
- Jews believe that marriage is the natural state for humans and the place to bring up children. So it is an expectation of all Jews to marry and have children.
- Marriage is a blessing from God.
- It helps an individual to overcome loneliness.
- It is seen as the 'completion' of each other for the couple.

The marriage ceremony in brief

- Takes place under a wedding canopy (*huppah*).
- The bride and groom recite blessings over wine, and exchange rings.
- Then the *ketubah* (marriage contract) is signed before witnesses.
- Then the rabbi gives a speech about marriage, followed by further blessings.
- After sharing a glass of wine, the groom crushes a glass underfoot.
- Finally the couple share some private time.

There are different cultural traditions

- Before the ceremony: Orthodox couples don't see each other for a week before marriage; whereas for other Jews it is just the day before that they don't meet.
- Aufruf: on the Shabbat morning before the wedding, Orthodox grooms are called to read the Torah in the synagogue. They are showered with sweets and nuts to symbolise that their sins are forgiven and all is good.
- Kabbalat Panim: Orthodox Jews have separate receptions before the wedding for men and women. The groom is toasted for health and happiness. The bride sits on a throne to greet guests. The mother-in-law breaks some pottery to show damage cannot be repaired so marriages must be worked at.
- Veiling the bride: Ashkenazi brides are personally veiled by the groom until after reaching the huppah. This recalls two stories – first, that Rebecca was veiled before marrying Isaac; second, that Jacob was tricked into marrying Leah when he should have married Rachel because she was veiled and so unseen by him. In Reform and Masorti traditions, the bride places a kippah on the groom's head or cloaks him with tallit.
- Circling the huppah – Orthodox Jews do this seven times, others do it three times.

Death and mourning

For Jews, the mourning period is very much about supporting the bereaved, making them see they are not alone. While a person mourns, their community rallies round.

1. The person dies	2. Burial
The dead person's eyes are closed – this is to close off this life, allowing them to see the next life. The body is covered and placed on the ground. Candles are lit and placed at the head. The body will be watched until burial when the soul departs, no one knows when the soul leaves the body, hence the kindness of sitting with the body. The body is prepared for death by the hevrah kadishah, washed, dressed in white linen. Men are wrapped in their tallit, with the tzitzit removed (they are no longer bound by the mitzvot).	Burial happens as soon as possible after death, and they are interred in a wooden casket. Keria'ah ritual sees the mourners' garments torn or a strip of black ribbon worn. The casket is carried to the grave with seven stops along the way. It is lowered into the grave, with the head facing east (towards Jerusalem). The prayer of mercy is recited. The grave is filled by those present to show service and love. Men form lines for the bereaved to pass through. A meal is provided by friends and neighbours as a form of comfort.
3. Mourning	**4. Remembering the dead**
Aninut – between death and burial the bereaved are excused from all religious duties. Shiv'ah – seven days after burial for parents or children. You sit on low stools and are not allowed to work. Aninut still applies. People visit after three days to comfort, bring gifts and say prayers. It is common to take food to the bereaved – the community looks after them. Sheloshim – 30 days (including the seven days) some restrictions lifted, i.e. work can be resumed. Avelut – the next 11 months mourning continues for a parent. Mourners' kiddush recited at synagogue to help the dead be released from any sins.	Families must buy a gravestone so that the dead cannot be forgotten. Yahrzeit is the anniversary of the death of a parent. Fasting is done. A memorial candle is lit for 24 hours. Donations of tzedakah are made. The Yizkor memorial prayer is recited by mourners on special days in the year.

Some differences

- Funerals can take place at the grave, at a synagogue, at the funeral home.
- Those in attendance at the funeral will make a tear in their clothes (Orthodox), or wear a black ribbon (Reform).

Now test yourself

1 Describe a marriage ceremony.
2 Why is it important?
3 Describe a funeral.
4 Describe the mourning period in Judaism.

Jewish dietary law

- **Kashrut** means people and actions that cover Jewish religious requirements.
- The requirements are laid down mainly in Leviticus 11 and Deuteronomy 14.
- Jewish people must keep **kosher** – a set of rules about animals that are 'fit' or acceptable to eat. Food not fit to eat or unclean is **treyfah**.
- Acceptable animals must be slaughtered in the correct way to maintain kosher.
- Not all parts of kosher animals are kosher to eat.
- Basic kosher principles are – animals that have both split hooves (feet) and chew the cud (eat grass), fish with fins and scales, clean birds (poultry) i.e. those which do not consume other creatures are acceptable. Pigs are considered unclean. Any animal that has died naturally cannot be eaten (as it won't have been ritually slaughtered). Eggs also have to be checked as some have a blood spot in them.
- Vegetables are a neutral food (**parev**) so are fine after being washed clean to eat with anything.
- There are rules about not eating milk and meat products together.
- The rules also cover food preparation and use of cooking implements.
- Dietary laws are observed differently by Jews today – some loosely, some strictly.
- Jews often have separate sinks, fridges, cupboards, pans and utensils to keep meat and milk separate. This in effect means a double kitchen which many Jews cannot afford or fit in their house, but many strictly Orthodox Jews do this to the letter of the law.
- Keeping kosher is part of being Jewish, reminding them of their connection with God who is their creator.

Kashrut is the term used to denote Jewish food law.

Kosher means acceptable to eat.

Treyfah means unclean or unfit to eat.

Parev refers to neutral food.

Shochet is a qualified kosher slaughterer.

Some differences

- Many Jews keep a strict kosher diet using Jewish butchers and shops, for example, many Jews only lightly observe kashrut though, for example, not scrutinising packets to check the contents are kosher, or even eating non-kosher foods.
- Some Jews will have one set of dishes and kitchen utensils, which they ritually clean for Pesach; most have two sets (one just for Pesach).
- The cuisine of Ashkenazi Jews is quite different from that of Sephardi Jews. Ashkenazi is based on heavy stews (food for a northern European climate), whereas Sephardi is based on 'small bites' (the meze style of southern Europe).

Commentaries on Exam Practice answers at **www.hoddereducation.co.uk/myrevisionnotes**

Ritual slaughter

- Two key criteria – the animal must be one allowed by scripture and have been slaughtered in the right way.
- An animal must have been killed by the *shochet*, using a sharp blade to cut the neck with one stroke of the blade. This causes quick blood loss and death – humane for the animal.
- Kosher butchers are regulated by the **bet din**.

Draining of blood

- Blood is the life of the animal ('For the life of the flesh is in the blood' Leviticus, 17:11) and is forbidden to Jews.
- The *shochet* will remove most of the blood from the meat.
- Within 72 hours of slaughter the rest of the blood is removed by **broiling**, soaking or salting the meat.
- Most meat has had this done by the butcher but many Jews still salt meat before cooking.

Meat and milk

- The Torah commands 'Do not boil a kid in its mother's milk.'
- The Talmud explains this as there should be no cooking or eating of the mixture of meat and milk.
- There must be no meat and milk in the same meal or within six hours of each other.
- It is believed this act shows compassion as to have a mother seeing their child or vice versa being cooked and eaten would be cruel – hence providing dignity and sanctity to both lives.

Jewish cuisine

- Cuisine varies according to region, and is influenced by the culture within which it develops.
- Ashkenazi Jews based in north-east Europe have very distinctive food from Sephardi Jews based in Spain and the Mediterranean.

Issues of living in a non-Jewish country

Most Jews live outside Israel so it is not surprising that in other countries they often live in large Jewish communities making it possible to access kosher foods. There is still the issue of non-kosher meat and foods on display and being served everywhere outside their community, though.

> **Now test yourself**   TESTED ☐
>
> 1 Explain kosher and treyfah.
> 2 Why do Jews observe dietary law?
> 3 How do Jews observe dietary law?

Exam tip

Remember that there are no 'describe' questions on your exam so you need to know the above information and be able to apply it. You must be able to show the impact it has on Jewish life. For example, to explain two ways in which keeping kosher is important in a Jew's life. The answer would focus on why kosher is important, not what it is.

Bet din is a rabbinical court, the remit of which includes checking kosher butchers, and awarding kosher status.

Broiling is to cook something by direct heat.

Festivals: Rosh Hashanah – Jewish new year

- The High Holy Day on the first day of the month of Tishri beginning a 10-day period of reflection and repentance.
- The focus is on individuals' behaviour on earth (keeping commandments).
- The festival represents the day of creation. Jews believe all people will stand before God to be judged on actions in past year. Hoping to receive mercy, the next 10 days are a chance to make sure of it.
- Jews believe the righteous gain another year, the wicked do not and others have the chance over Rosh Hashanah to make repentance and secure another year.

Some differences

- Orthodox Jews observe Rosh Hashanah for two days; many Reform Jews for just one.
- While it is common to eat challah bread, or apples dipped in honey before the Rosh Hashanah meal, some Jews also eat pomegranates (the seeds reflecting the number of good deeds to be done in the next year).

Customs

- A special midnight service on the Shabbat before Rosh Hashanah.
- The shofar is blown – a call to repentance.
- Tashlich; recited and the bread (sins) thrown into the water in the hope that God will forgive.
- The first night is dedicated to prayer, meditation and soul-searching.
- Celebration meals take place using sweet things like honey.

Beliefs and importance for Jews today

- There is repentance and mercy sought for lapses of faith and behaviour.
- To show they deserve more time on earth as their lives are productive and actions are good.
- No one is so far away from God that they cannot find their way back to him.
- It highlights that deeds on earth are very important – rather than a focus on the afterlife.
- Carrying out *tikkun olam* and keeping the commandments are essential.

Festivals: Yom Kippur

- This is the Day of Atonement and is referred to in Leviticus 'to cleanse from sins'.
- It is a day of confession – to cast out sins and make heartfelt resolutions to sin no more.
- The day brings pardon from God; forgiveness only comes if there is an attempt to repair any damage.

Events

- Kol Nidre service takes place – the prayer asks for release from all pledges to God, recognising that not all promises made can be kept.
- There is a day of fasting (25 hours) – a difficult one but they should be cheerful. White garments worn.

- On this day the book of life closes so they gain another year – they thank God for being loving and merciful for releasing all their sin.
- All synagogue services have the theme of confession and repentance.

Beliefs and importance for Jews today

- It is the completion of a year – like a new start.
- Being truly repentant is important.
- It shows that everyone can find their way back to God.
- The atonement on this day is about sins between man and God rather than sins between each other (these have to be put right before Yom Kippur).

Festivals: Pesach

Pesach is a festival of joy and all Jewish traditions celebrate in the same way. It is one of the three pilgrim festivals where every Jew had to attend Temple for sacrifice. It is celebrated for seven days in Israel, or eight outside of Israel. The festival today reinforces key customs which have enriched home life, as well as emphasising the religion and its links with history.

Origins

- It remembers the Israelite people taken out of slavery in Egypt 3,000 years ago.
- Belief that God will always come to the rescue is essential; Pesach is an example of this.
- Jews appreciate that the freedoms they have today were given by God, and that they should fight for freedom for all.
- There is the hope of 'Next Year in Jerusalem', which is the hope that Jerusalem will be rebuilt as the spiritual centre of the world.

Preparing for Pesach

- The morning before Pesach, the firstborn son attends synagogue to study a portion of the Talmud.
- Most Jews give to charity (*maot chitim*).
- Chametz is removed, which means that the ten pieces of bread that have been hidden round the house the previous evening by the father and children, are found, wrapped and burnt before Pesach starts.
- Homes are spring-cleaned, new clothes are bought, special meals are prepared so that the occasion is joyful.

The seder meal

- It is held on the first or second night of Pesach following instructions from the Haggadah Book (which tells the story of the Israelites and the Passover).
- This Book provides readings, hymns of thanks, symbolic explanations of scripture and a song of divine retribution which God brings for the mistreatment of the Israelites.
- The leader of the meal wears a *kittel* (white linen gown), which celebrates freedom from the Egyptians.

- The table is set with three matzah, wine and the seder plate.
- The matzah is unleavened to remember the Israelites not having time to bake bread before they escaped Egypt.
- On the Seder plate *maror* represents the enslavement of the Israelites, *karpas* (vegetables) represents the tears of the slaves, *charoset* represents the mortar made by the Israelite slaves, the shank bone represents the mighty arm of God and the paschal lamb represents sacrifice and a roasted egg represents the Temple sacrifice.
- Wine is drunk and 10 drops are spilled representing the 10 plagues.
- An extra cup is set for Elijah (to be used if a stranger turns up). Elijah is a reminder of the Messianic Age.
- The door is opened twice at the end of the meal to show the belief in the protection of God from harmful forces.

Key concepts of Pesach

- Memory – the past gives Jewish lives purpose/meaning and a better future.
- Hope – without it the Israelites would not have survived.
- Faith – the Jews are blessed with support from a caring God, giving optimism for self, now and in the future.
- Family – learning about the past strengthens the sense of belonging to the faith.
- Responsibility to others – the experience of the Israelites shows Jews need to care for those in need.

Now test yourself

1 Give the names of some Jewish festivals and what they celebrate.
2 Why is Rosh Hashanah important?
3 Give some of the symbols of Rosh Hashanah.
4 What are the key elements of Yom Kippur?
5 Describe a seder meal.
6 What are the symbols of the seder plate?

TESTED ☐

Theme A: Religion, relationships and families

Relationships and the human condition – love and sexuality: communion and complementarity

Humans as sexual, male and female

The Genesis creation stories tell us:
- that humanity is made in the **image of God**
- that God made both male and female
- that God intended humans to procreate (have children).

Jesus' teaching about **marriage** reinforces this. In St Mark's Gospel he said that people are made male and female, and God intended them to be joined in marriage. Men and women are designed to be complementary, making up what each other lacks.

Catholic teaching about sexual love

Catholics believe human sexuality is more than a mechanism that allows for the continuation of the species, but also as a divine gift. They believe that sexual love is marital, unitive and procreative.

The Catholic Church regards both pre-marital sex (sex before marriage) and extra-marital sex (sex with someone other than your husband or wife) wrong, as sexual relationships should be within the commitment of marriage.

Marital

The Catholic Church says that sex should only happen within marriage. The sacrament of marriage is a commitment of love between a man and a woman and the vows said by the bride and groom are the central part of the ceremony or rite. A marriage has to be **consummated** by sexual intercourse for it to be seen as valid.

Unitive

Sexual love is unitive as it brings two people together, becoming 'one' (Mark 10:8). Adultery is seen as wrong as this breaks this unity and bond of trust.

Procreative

Catholics believe that every sexual act should be **procreative**. Catholic couples are expected to raise children as the fruit of their marriage and their love.

From the above, it can be seen that sex is not just for having children, but is an important part of a loving relationship and union.

> **Image of God** is the dignity of human beings shown as they share some of God's attributes such as reason and love. The Catholic Church recommends the refined methods of self-observation
>
> **Marriage** is the sacrament in which a man and a woman pledge their love to each other for life.
>
> **Consummated** means completed; in marriage it means the act of sexual intercourse.
>
> **Procreative** means open to producing new life, having children.

> According to God's will, husband and wife should encounter each other in bodily union so as to be united even more deeply with one another in love and to allow children to proceed from their love.' (*YouCat*, 417)

Pope John Paul II's *Theology of the Body*

Pope John Paul II gave a series of talks about the human body and relationships. The central idea is that the human body, male and female, is not inferior to the spiritual but a visible expression of it. As John Paul II said 'the body, and it alone, is capable of making visible what is invisible: the spiritual and the divine. It was created to transfer into the visible reality of the world the mystery hidden since time immemorial in

Commentaries on Exam Practice answers at **www.hoddereducation.co.uk/myrevisionnotes**

God, and thus be a sign of it.' The Creator has given humanity bodies and spirits/individual personalities, that work together as part of a whole.

- The body is not inferior to the personality but feelings and thoughts are expressed through it.
- Men and women are created equal in dignity and made for relationships.
- The body is fully expressed in a loving relationship with the opposite sex. This is what he called 'the **nuptial** meaning of the body.'
- Marriage is a **communion** of persons, and in sexual intercourse, they give themselves totally to one another.
- Sexual relationships are good, but within the committed relationship of marriage.

- **Extramarital** sex turns what should be a sign of mutual love and commitment into something selfish and just for personal pleasure.
- Adultery breaks trust and the bond of marriage, breaking a promise made, hence it is an injustice.
- The openness to new life through the sex act is part of the whole process. Human bodies are designed to create life and thus artificial means of contraception are an interference and an interruption of the natural law.

> **Nuptial** is something to do with a marriage.
>
> **Communion** is sharing love and communication together.
>
> **Extramarital** means sex outside marriage.

Contrasting views

REVISED

Society today has varied views on human sexuality and marriage.

Issues	Catholic view	Other Christian views	Other views
Sex before marriage	Catholics believe that sex should only take place within marriage.	Most other Christian groups accept that sex belongs in marriage but also accept artificial contraception.	Many people wait until they have met someone they really like, or love, to have sex. Others engage in more casual sex. Humanists believe that people should have personal freedom to choose when to have sex, as long as their decision does not cause harm.
Adultery	Catholics believe that adultery is wrong because it breaks trust and the bond of marriage, breaking a promise made, hence it is an injustice.	Other Christian groups think adultery is wrong because it breaks the marriage vows and destroys the trust between a couple.	Most people, agnostics, humanists or atheists would also see it as wrong for it breaks trust and commitment.
Homosexuality	The Catholic Church does not condemn anyone for being homosexual and recognises that such an orientation does exist. Yet the Church cannot bless sexual relationships between people of the same sex as it believes sex should be able to result in children.	Most other Christian groups do not accept same-sex marriage but support civil partnerships. Some individuals do accept same-sex marriage, though.	Secular society accepts sexual relationships, and same-sex marriage was made legal in England and Wales in 2014. However, people do have differing views on this, some feeling that marriage should be between a man and a woman, with others believing same-sex couples should have the same rights as anyone else. Humanists support the rights of same-sex couples.

Now test yourself

TESTED

1 State two things that Genesis teaches about human beings.
2 What three things does the Catholic Church teach about marriage?
3 Find and explain two points in Pope John Paul II's *Theology of the Body*.
4 Why does the Church say that adultery is wrong?

Perspectives on relationships – marriage, cohabitation, divorce and separation

Valid marriage in the Catholic Church

For a **marriage** to be official in the eyes of the Catholic Church it has to meet certain criteria:
- The couple are free to marry – not already married or under vows of celibacy such as priests or monks, or not too closely related like brothers and sisters or first cousins.
- They marry of their own free will without any pressure.
- The intend to marry for life and be open to having children.
- They are married in front of a Catholic priest or deacon with the Church's rites and blessing.
- The marriage is only finally valid when consummated – the couple have sex.

Marriage, according to the Church, is a covenant, a sacred agreement and union between a man and a woman. This is for mutual support and for the procreation of children. It is seen as a sacrament, an action that conveys a spiritual blessing, for Christ made it so by his presence at the wedding in Cana. A sacrament is given once and cannot be undone, so long as it is validly performed.

> The matrimonial covenant, by which a man and a woman establish between themselves a partnership of the whole of life, is by its nature ordered towards the good of the offspring: this covenant between baptised persons has been raised by Christ the Lord to the dignity of a sacrament. (*Catechism of the Catholic Church*, 1,601)

Marriage vows

The exchange of vows during the wedding service is when the couple become married. The vows are the promises the couples make to each other:
- These are about the promise of commitment to each other for life, 'for richer, for poorer, in sickness and in health, to love and to cherish, till death us do part.'
- The couple make the vows when joining their hands.
- The wedding rings are a symbol of the vows. The circle is about lasting forever and the gift is about the gift of love.

Catholic views on annulment, divorce and remarrying

Annulment

Annulment is a decision taken by the Church that no valid marriage ever took place, though its ceremony did. There are various reasons why an annulment might be given:
- One partner had various affairs and so did not respect the marriage vows.
- The couple never had sex.
- The couple always used contraception and never intended to have children.
- One partner was coerced into marriage against their will.
- One or both partners were not mature enough to really give their considered consent.

> **Marriage** in the Catholic Church is seen as a binding sacrament for life.
>
> **Annulment** is when a marriage is said to have never been valid.
>
> **Divorce** is the ending of a marriage legally.

Divorce

The state law allows **divorce** to end a marriage and then the people are free to remarry. The Catholic Church does not accept this because:
- the couple made life long vows
- they were united in a sacrament that cannot be broken, becoming 'one flesh'
- Jesus taught that anyone who divorces and marries another is committing adultery.

However, the Church recognises that sometimes relationships break down and in some circumstances divorce is necessary for legal and financial reasons. However, if either person wants to remarry in the Catholic Church they will also need to get an annulment.

Different ethical views on divorce

Ethical arguments against divorce	Ethical arguments for divorce
The marriage vows are sacred and blessed by God – so they should not be broken.	Sometimes relationships break down and cannot be repaired. To force the couple to stay together would cause them a lot of suffering.
Jesus taught that divorce followed by remarriage was the same as adultery.	Jesus taught compassion and love for your neighbour and in this case the compassionate thing to do is allow divorce.
This is the view of the Catholic Church.	

Remarriage

Remarriage is getting married again having already been married.
- When a spouse dies, the marriage is seen to end in the eyes of the Church and a widow or widower is free to remarry.
- When an annulment is granted, a person is free to marry as the first marriage is declared null and void.

> **Remarriage** is getting married again after having already married.

Different attitudes

Different attitudes to cohabitation

Cohabitation is when a couple live together, maybe for many years, without being married. Many non-religious people see no problem with cohabitation, believing it gives couples a chance to see if they are compatible before committing to marry. Cohabitation is the fastest growing family type in the UK. Some people may live together before they get married while others may never marry and continue to live together. The Catholic Church does not agree with cohabitation because it believes cohabitation lacks the commitment of a marriage.

Christians in general do not support or encourage cohabitation. However, pastors and ministers tend to not condemn but encourage partners to get married.

Attitudes to same-sex marriage

Since 2004, same-sex couples could enter in to civil partnerships in the UK, and in 2014 same-sex marriage was legalised in the UK.
However, there are different views on the subject:
- The Catholic Church believes that marriage is part of the order of creation where men and women are created for complementary and biologically designed to procreate (have children). It therefore does not agree with same-sex marriage because it is not open to procreation,

though it is against discrimination and hatred towards homosexual people.
- Some other Christians think same-sex marriage is a matter of justice and equality. These individuals and groups do not always understand marriage as a sacrament like the Catholic Church.
- Many non-religious people, including humanists, believe that same-sex people should be entitled to the same rights as heterosexual couples.

> They [homosexual people] must be accepted with respect, compassion and sensitivity. Every sign of unjust discrimination in their regard should be avoided. (*Catechism of the Catholic Church*, 2,358)

Now test yourself

1 Give two of the criteria the Catholic Church needs to see in a couple to celebrate a valid marriage.
2 Why is marriage described as a covenant?
3 Which part of the rite of marriage actually marries the couple?
4 Explain what annulment means and give one example that can allow this to happen.
5 If a Catholic gets divorced and remains single, will they be allowed to receive communion?

Families and responsibilities – roles of men, women and children

Catholics and family planning

REVISED

Family planning means controlling how many children you have and when you have them. Couples can control this with natural methods, for example, not having sex at certain times of the month, or artificial methods like condoms or the birth control pill.

Catholic views about family planning are based on their beliefs about marriage:

- The Catholic understanding of marriage is a commitment and sex within this should be both unitive and procreative. Catholics do not agree with the use of artificial contraception, because it is seen as separating the two aspects of sexual intercourse.
- The Church does teach responsible parenthood, though, and does not expect each family to have numerous children. **Natural family planning** (NFP) is taught; this is where the couple maps the woman's fertile periods each month and doesn't have sex during these times. This is seen as working with nature and not stopping pregnancy artificially by interfering with the natural process.
- Pope Paul VI reaffirmed the Church's teaching in *Humanae vitae* in 1968. He feared that artificial contraception, particularly the contraceptive pill would lead to increased promiscuity and the possibility that the state could limit how many children couples could have (as happened in China).

> **Natural family planning** (NFP) is observing changes in the woman's body to show infertile periods.
>
> **Procreation** means to have children.

> The Catholic Church recommends the refined methods of self-observation and natural family planning (NFP) as methods of deliberately regulating conception [...] they demand mutual affection and consideration and therefore are a school of love. (*YouCat*, 421)

Different perspectives on the use of artificial contraception

- Some Catholics think that some forms of artificial contraception should be allowed within marriage.
- Other Christian groups such as the Church of England accept artificial contraception and though children are a gift from God, it is up to the couple whether to have them and when.
- Many non-religious people, including humanists, support the use of artificial contraception. It is better to use contraception to prevent having children than to have children who aren't wanted or can't be well cared for.

The nature and purpose of the family

REVISED

The Catholic Church sees the family as the domestic Church where God is served. The family also takes their place within the wider parish family. Catholics view the purpose of the family as follows:

- **Procreation** – The family is the best and most stable environment to bring up children.
- **Security** – Children can grow and learn within a stable environment, accepted by the parents and interacting with their siblings.
- **Education** – Parents will teach their children about many parts of life and will educate them

about the Christian faith. The parents have authority but also must have compassion.

Contrasting views

Many people now live in family units that are not the typical 'nuclear family' of a mother, father and children. Single parent families are widespread because of divorce and many couples cohabit rather than marry. There is also the right for homosexual couples to adopt (and to marry).

The roles and responsibilities of men and women

Biblical teaching, such as the writings of St Paul in his letter to the Ephesians (Ephesians 5:21–6:4), suggests that the man is head of the household and a wife should be submissive. This was typical of social attitudes when the Bible was written but would be seen as discriminatory by many today.

However, St Paul also taught that a husband should love his wife as himself and that while wives should obey their husbands, their husbands should treat them with respect.

The dignity of work in the home

- Traditionally the mother raises the children and runs the home and the father goes out to work. The Catholic Church values both types of work equally and believes both have dignity.
- While the Catholic Church would affirm and praise the traditional role of the mother if that is what a family desires, it is also recognised that many wives might want to work, to be fulfilled through developing and exercising their gifts, or might need to work.

The rights of same-sex couples or single parents to have children

- A single person may adopt, but this would not usually be ideal as it would be better for a child to have two parents if at all possible.
- Same-sex couples can adopt legally and argue that very caring and committed relationships can be excellent for raising children. The Catholic Church teaches that children should be adopted in heterosexual families as the role for the mother and father should be present. This causes less confusion in the child as they are growing up, and also a balance of care. (Some individual Catholics question this, but the Church as a whole takes this stance.) Other Christians sometimes accept same-sex couples adopting children if they are in a committed, loving relationship.
- Sometimes two men wanting to bring up a child together pay to use the technology of IVF. This involves a complex procedure in which a donated egg is fertilised and implanted in the womb of a woman who has agreed to bring the baby into the world. Catholic teaching would find this procedure unethical.

> The Christian family [...] is the first community called to announce the Gospel to the human person during growth and to bring him or her, through a progressive education and catechesis [sharing of the faith], to full human and Christian maturity. (*Familiaris consortio* 1)

Now test yourself

1 Does the Catholic Church allow family planning? If so, explain how.
2 What did Pope Paul VI warn about artificial contraception in *Humane vitae*?
3 What three purposes of the family are taught by the Catholic Church?
4 What is the attitude of the Catholic Church to the roles of men and women in the family?
5 What is the attitude of the Catholic Church to same-sex marriage?

TESTED

Theme A: Religion, relationships and families

Dialogue 4: Gender, equality and discrimination – equality between men and women

Women and men in the Biblical tradition

There are many parts of the Bible that would support the **equality** of men and women:

● Genesis 1 says that men and women are both created in the image of God.
● In Genesis 2, God may have created Eve from Adam but the point is made that they are equal as both are human beings.
● Various important women feature in the Bible such as Deborah who is described as a leader and a judge in ancient Israel or Esther who was married to the Persian king.
● Mary is seen as the most important woman in the Bible as the mother of Jesus and the perfect disciple.
● The risen Jesus appeared first to some of the women, particularly Mary of Magdala. This was unheard of at the time, as women could not be recognised as reliable and legal witnesses.

However, men dominate the Bible, though, for that was the culture of the time. Most of the prophets were male, and the 12 disciples were male.

> **Equality** is when all people have the same dignity and rights.
>
> **Prejudice** is judging something before all the facts are known or understood.
>
> **Discrimination** means to treat people unfairly and differently when they do not deserve it.

Catholics teaching on the equality of women and men

● The Catholic Church teaches that men and women are equal as they were both made in the image of God.
● However, equality does not mean they are exactly the same. There are differences between men and women. For example only a woman can be a mother and only a man can impregnate a woman.
● Neither men nor women are higher in status than the other. Their roles are complementary and support each other. When the Church says that only men can be priests, it is because Jesus was male, and not because they think there is anything inferior about women.

Other views

Many people would say that belief in equality of men and women means that they should have the same opportunities as they are equally capable of doing the same jobs. So women should have the opportunity to take what would traditionally have been men's roles, for example working outside the home, and men should have the opportunity to do traditionally female roles, being a stay at home dad for example.

Gender prejudice and discrimination

Gender **prejudice** is when assumptions are made about someone based on their gender, these might include:

- There are certain jobs that are for men (builder, banker) and certain jobs that are for women (secretary, nurse).
- That men will make better leaders than women.
- That women are more emotional and caring than men.

Gender **discrimination** means acting in a certain way towards someone based on your prejudice, this might include:

- Not giving men or women certain jobs.
- Paying women less than a man to do the same job.
- Overlook women for promotion and promote men instead even if they have the same qualifications.

The Catholic Church teaches the following:

- Gender discrimination is opposed by the Catholic Church as men and women are created equal.
- Refusal to give women certain jobs, or to pay them equal wages is condemned by the Church.
- Women should have the right and protection to be mothers in the home rather than seeing outside employment if they wish to; the Church sees this as a God given right.
- Adequate social care and child care, as well as family benefits are needed to allow mothers to stay at home in some cases.
- Men and women still have their differences though. Thus only men can be ordained priests. Secular society sees this as gender discrimination.

> The Christian family [...] is the first community called to announce the Gospel to the human person during growth and to bring him or her, through a progressive education and catechesis [sharing of the faith], to full human and Christian maturity. (*Familiaris consortio* 1)
>
> In the 'unity of the two', man and woman are called from the beginning not only to exist 'side by side' or 'together'; but they are also called to exist mutually 'one for the other'. (*Mulieris dignitatem* 7)
>
> Why is it expected that women must earn less than men? No! They have the same rights. The disparity is a pure scandal. (Pope Francis)

Now test yourself

1 Explain one part of the Bible that teaches the dignity and importance of women.
2 Why can only men be priests in the Catholic Church if the Church believes in equality?
3 What does the Church teach about the roles of men and women in society?
4 Explain gender discrimination and give one example of the Church's response to it.

Theme B: Religion, peace and conflict

Christian perspectives on human violence, justice, forgiveness and reconciliation

Biblical perspectives on violence

- The creation stories in Genesis make it clear that God's intention is for peace and harmony.
- However, Genesis also contains stories that show that humans can be selfish and violent. For example the story of Cain who kills his brother Abel (Genesis, 4:5–11).
- Jesus was a model of non-violence in many ways, such as teaching that people should 'turn the other cheek' and how he went to the cross, and did not argue with Pilate.
- Jesus, in the Sermon on the Mount, identified violence as being caused by feelings of anger inside a person. They need to be aware of this and seek to forgive.

Bullying

The charity Bullying UK says bullying is repeated behaviour designed to hurt someone emotionally or physically. Bullying can take many forms:
- verbal (e.g. name calling/threats)
- physical (e.g. assault)
- social (e.g. ignoring someone or leaving them out of a group)
- cyber-bullying (e.g. sending cruel messages via social media, posting embarrassing photos of someone).

In the Scriptures, James says that the tongue and words spoken can do great damage to other people, thus people should be careful how they speak to others. For Catholics, bullying is wrong because each person is made in the image of God and so deserves respect.

Forgiveness

Forgiveness is the letting go of guilt and anger with yourself or someone else. Jesus practised this when he:
- prayed for those nailing him on to the cross (Luke 23:34)
- forgave Peter for denying knowing him (John 21:15–17)

- taught that there was no limit to how many times a person could be forgiven (Matthew 18:21-22)
- taught us to pray the Our Father 'And forgive us our trespasses, as we forgive those who trespass against us.'
- told the parable of the Unforgiving Servant, about the need to forgive enemies (Matthew 18:23–35).

Reconciliation

Reconciliation is where two people, or groups, make peace. It is a bringing back together. Understanding and empathy are needed, understanding why a problem has arisen and feeling sympathy for the people who have been hurt and angry.

The Catholic Church believes in encouraging forgiveness and reconciliation as without them there can be no peace. Pope Francis, travelling the world, often calls for reconciliation.
- In John 14:27, Jesus says that he gives his peace, a peace that society ('the world') cannot give.

Christians are therefore called to be different in how they act towards others, and work for reconciliation.

Forgiveness is letting off the wrong someone has done to you.

Justice is fairness in the treatment of all people.

Reconciliation is bringing broken relationships back together again.

Justice and human dignity

Justice means treating people fairly. The Scriptures make it clear that justice extremely important, and that worship is not acceptable to God unless people live fairly and justly (Amos 5:23–24). The Church works for justice as one way of extending the Kingdom of God.

Injustice can cause people to become hopeless or angry and make it hard to achieve peace. One modern example is the Middle East conflict between Israelis and Palestinians where both sides have hurt one another and violence can break out on both sides in different ways.

> But let justice roll down like waters, and righteousness like an ever-flowing stream.' (Amos 5:24)

Righteous anger

There might be times and situations when righteous anger is needed to help stop injustice. Jesus used this when he drove money changers out of the Jerusalem Temple (John 2:13–17). Great care should be taken with this for it is too easy to react in anger out of the emotion of the moment and make matters worse.

- The Catholic Church accepts that some conflict is sometimes necessary for the sake of justice. This should avoid violence wherever possible. The development of concepts such as the 'just war' theory reflect this view.
- Most other Christians accept this, too. However, some are total pacifists.
- Non-religious groups agree that anger is appropriate in some situations of injustice, with argument, protest and campaigns being needed. Sometimes violence might be the only way for some. Non-violent protest is a tradition that some secular people would use, even though this is based upon Hindu ideas and also Christian ones.

> Building a just social and civil order, wherein each person receives what is his or her due, is an essential task which every generation must take up anew.' (*Deus caritas est*, 28)
>
> Father of orphans and protector of widows is God in his holy habitation. (Psalm 68:5)

Violent protest

Protest is when someone takes action to express their anger at injustice, it could be legal peaceful protest, for example, marches, or might involve illegal violent action. An example of a successful protest would be the Suffragettes at the start of the twentieth century campaigning for votes for women. A recent example of protest would be demonstrations against fracking in the UK.

Violent protest is illegal in the UK and not supported by the Church, but there are occasions when individuals feel that they have no option because nothing else could stop an injustice. It is dangerous, for violence can lead to more violence.

- The Catholic Church would not always condemn all violence in the cause of justice as in the Just War theory but it must be an absolutely last resort.
- Other Christian groups would agree, basing their values on the gospel teachings of Jesus.
- Secular groups would not have the fears and moral limitations of the Church. Some would advocate violence to seek social change. It depends upon the group and the individual.

Now test yourself

1 What did Jesus teach was the origin of violence (verbal or physical) towards other people?
2 Give two examples of forgiveness from the New Testament.
3 Explain the difference between forgiveness and reconciliation.
4 How did Jesus once use violence and what is the name of the theory that allows Catholics to use violence in certain circumstances?

TESTED

Christian perspectives on social justice and just war

Just war theory

REVISED

The early Christians did not fight in wars or undertake military service. Jesus had told his disciples that those who live by the sword shall die by the sword, and to turn the other cheek when attacked.

> Those who wage war justly to aim at peace, and so they are not opposed to peace. Hence Augustine says: 'We do not seek peace in order to be at war, but we go to war that we may have peace. Be peaceful, therefore, in warring, so that you vanquish those whom you war against, and bring them to the prosperity of peace.' (St Thomas Aquinas, *Summa Theologica*)

When Christianity became the religion of the Roman Empire, Christians were expected to serve in the army and various tribal groups were invading. Thinkers such as St Augustine and later St Thomas Aquinas worked out the idea of the **just war theory**. This is a list of criteria a war must meet for it to be morally justified:

- War has to be a last resort after attempts to negotiate have failed.
- A war has to be declared by the rightful authority, e.g. a state.
- There must be a just cause.
- There has to be a good chance of success or more violence will be the result.
- Only proportionate force must be used so no weapons that would cause huge damage (for example nuclear weapons).
- Only the armed forces of either side should be involved, not innocent civilians.

Just war theory is the set of conditions to be followed for the Church to say a war is just.

Weapons of mass destruction (WMD) are nuclear weapons that can created massive damage.

So war is justified by the Church only when the incident is very serious and all other alternatives have been tried. The *Catechism of the Catholic Church* 2,309, says that these conditions must be met to ensure that any conflict has 'moral legitimacy'.

Conditions have changed since the days when Augustine and Aquinas were alive and we have new technology that could kill millions of people. This raises new moral issues.

Catholic attitudes to nuclear war and weapons of mass destruction

REVISED

Weapons of mass destruction (WMD) are weapons that can kill lots of people in one go. They can include:

- nuclear weapons – weapons that use nuclear reactions to generate huge amounts of energy that can kill thousands or even millions of people.
- chemical weapons – weapons that use poisonous chemicals to kill people
- biological weapons – weapons that use toxins like bacteria or viruses to kill people.

There are five main reasons why the Church opposes the use of WMD:

- Many innocent civilians will be killed, and there will be long-term effects.

- Their effect is disproportionate to the evils being resisted, because the destruction they cause is so severe.
- The possibility of anyone winning is very small. The likelihood is that all would suffer and much of the earth would be wasteland. Pope Benedict XVI said that there would be no 'victors, only victims' (Message for the World, Day of Peace).
- They are extremely expensive, with the UK Trident submarines and missiles costing billions for example. The money could be used for other things in society, such as health and medicine in the world.
- It can be argued that any nation that has WMD is seen as a potential threat to others and this increases tension.

Even if the use of WMD would give a good result the Catholic Church believes the death and destruction they cause could not be justified.

Contrasting views on WMD

Many (including some Catholics) feel that we must possess WMD as a deterrent against others using them.

Others, whether secular or religious, agree with the Catholic Church that possession of nuclear weapons is immoral and increases fear and tension. They feel that Britain should disarm and set an example to ease tension.

Catholic views of the consequences of modern warfare

REVISED

- **Civilian casualties**: The Catholic Church teaches that civilians must not be targeted during war, however, often wars result in civilians being wounded or killed. Catholics believe that every effort must be taken to protect them and help all who are wounded no matter their race, nationality or religion. The Missionaries of Charity, in India, for example, will help Muslims, Hindus and Christians who are sick, left homeless or caught up in racial tension.
- **Refugees**: Refugees have to flee war zones, often with few possessions. The Catholic Church believes that they should be given a welcome in any nation that is at peace as a humanitarian gesture.
- **Environmental damage**: Environmental damage can be caused by modern warfare such as chemical weapons and the burning or clearing of vast areas of fertile land or forest. The Catholic Church teaches that the care of the environment is essential as the Church believes in creation; it is seen as God's world. Human beings have responsibility with their reason and power over nature, to offer wise and caring stewardship.

> 'We cannot insist too much on the duty of giving foreigners a hospitable reception.' (Pope Paul VI, Populum progressio 67)

Now test yourself

TESTED

1 What view did the early Christians take about using violence?
2 Give any two conditions of the just war theory.
3 State any two reasons why Catholics oppose nuclear war.
4 Give one consequence of modern warfare.

Holy war and pacifism

Religion and belief as a cause for war

REVISED ☐

Does religion cause violence and wars? There are many examples from around the world where this would seem to be the case.

However, wars that seem to be fought about religion often are far more complex in their origin, involving politics, money and possession of land and resources. For example, rivalry between Sunni and Shia Muslims in Iraq is about more than religious teachings that differ; who is in control of the government and land are also issues. Religion is one aspect, but it isn't the whole story.

Holy war

A **holy war** is a war that is fought to support a religious cause. It will usually be controlled by a religious leader (rather than a government or state).

A Christian example of a holy war would be the Crusades fought between the 11th and 13th centuries. Christians went to the Holy Land (Jerusalem) to free it from Muslim control. The Pope blessed this. Years later, there are deep regrets about how some of the Crusaders behaved, slaughtering many innocent people and seeking wealth. The fighting was not just about faith.

> A **holy war** is a conflict called by a religious leader mainly for reasons of faith.
>
> **Pacifism** is refusing to fight in any war.
>
> **Peacemakers** are those who are trying to reduce tension which causes conflict.

Old Testament perspectives on war

REVISED ☐

- There are many stories of battles in the Old Testament. Theirs was the tribal way of life, centuries before Christ came. Different groups often fought each other if they were not the same race or religion. Yet the prophets taught that God desires peace above all, as described in Isaiah 2:4 where a future time is described where swords will be turned into ploughs.
- 'Eye for eye, tooth for tooth' (Exodus 21:24) is from the Old Testament and suggests violence can be used in response to violence. However, this was actually intended to ensure that punishments were proportionate to the crime committed. Thus violence could also be used in conflicts when thought necessary.

> [...] they shall beat their swords into ploughshares, and their spears into pruning hooks; nation shall not lift up sword against nation, neither shall they learn war any more. (Isaiah 2:4)

Religion in the twenty-first century conflicts

REVISED ☐

- Raising awareness of conflicts – Pope Francis works for peace in various places. He has brought Muslims, Jews and Christians together in prayer, and had a meeting with the Presidents of Israel and Palestine in 2014. Such gatherings for prayer and listening began with Pope John Paul II in Assisi in 1986.
- Helping to resolve conflicts – The Catholic bishops can speak out more boldly than other religious groups under the dictatorship in Eritrea, North Africa, only because the Church there provides much of the medical care and hospitals and thus they are tolerated because of their necessary charitable work.
- Helping the victims of war – Catholic agencies such as CAFOD as well as Aid to the Church in Need support those hurt by war. CAFOD, for example, helped orphans in Sierra Leone and Aid to the Church in Need raised funds for Syrian refugees.

Pacifism

Pacifism is the belief that violence and war are never justifiable in any circumstances. Pacifists might be involved in conflicts in other ways, for example, treating the wounded but they will never fight – they are called 'conscientious objectors'. Some Christians are pacifists, for example, the Quakers, and Pax Christi ('Peace of Christ') is a Catholic organisation set up after World War II to work for peace. However, there are different views on this subject:

- Christian pacifists may point to some of the teaching of Jesus such as 'if anyone strikes you on the right cheek, turn the other also' (Matthew 5:39) and 'Blessed are the **peacemakers**' (Matthew 5:9), a teaching that was based upon the life and non-violent actions of Jesus himself.
- Catholics believe that violent conflict should be avoided unless as a last resort, and only then within strict limits as outlined in the just war theory. (Some Catholics are pacifists and the Church recognises their right to their conscience over this.) Priests and religious people (monks, friars and nuns) should not take arms and be involved in violent struggle.
- Some Humanists are pacifists believing that this respects all human life. War is always destructive and no one can keep in complete control of what happens within such a conflict. Modern weapons cause huge destruction and many civilians are unfortunately involved. Others accept warfare as a last resort if all other methods of reconciliation have been exhausted.

Papal teaching about pacifism

While the Church teaches that war can be justified in certain situations, there is respect for pacifism and the right of conscientious objection. This is shown, for example, in the Vatican II document, *The Church in the Modern World* and also repeated in the US bishops' *The Challenge of Peace* in 1983. Various popes have appealed for peace:

- Pope Benedict XV in 1917 with his Peace Note, calling on the European powers to stop fighting and seek a truce. He opposed any desire to inflict total defeat on other nations and warned that any acts of revenge would increase the likelihood of future wars (as it did with the rise of Adolf Hitler).
- Pope John XXIII spoke out in the encyclical, *Pacem in Terris* (Peace on Earth) in 1963, arguing against the immortality of nuclear weapons and the arms race. The Cuban missile crisis had ended the year before with the standoff between the USA and the USSR. 'We beg all governments not to remain deaf to this cry of humanity.'
- Pope Francis spoke movingly during his address in St Peter's Square on the hundredth anniversary of World War I; 'Please stop! I ask you with all my heart, it's time to stop. Stop, please!'

Now test yourself

1 What did Isaiah predict about war and peace?
2 Give one example of how the Catholic Church tries to help resolve conflicts.
3 How did Pope Benedict XV try to promote peace in 1917?
4 What was taught in *Pacem in Terris*?

Christian perspectives on terrorism and Christian initiatives in conflict resolution and peace making

Terrorism has its roots in social injustice and unrest where marginalised people turn to violence to change society and to be heard. However, they use violence against innocent civilians to instil fear, terror and to push for change. For Christians, this is not acceptable as it is a crime against humanity, and is against the teachings and life of Jesus.

Biblical perspectives

REVISED

- St Paul urges obedience to the authorities so that society can be peaceful. St Paul also advised that people did not take vengeance into their own hands, but trust God to come to their aid (Romans 12:19).
- The Catholic Church today opposes any form of terrorism and Pope Francis has often spoken out against terrorism activities in the name of God.
- While terrorism is to be condemned, the root causes and the injustice that may underlie this must also be honestly faced up to and debated.

This was the case with recent conflicts such as in Northern Ireland with the activities of the Irish Republican Army, shooting and bombing.
- Several terrorist attacks in recent years have been linked to Islamic extremists. The vast majority of Muslims have condemned these attacks and Catholic cardinals have stood alongside the Muslim community to pray with them, show solidarity and improve co-operation between the different faiths.

Catholic views on the use of torture

REVISED

Torture is illegal but some corrupt governments and extremist movements can use torture as a way of getting information, or of humiliating and punishing their opponents. Some people argue that torture is justified in extreme circumstances to gain important information that might save the lives of many.

The Catholic Church condemns all use of torture. It denies people of their basic human rights, and this is wrong even if they have denied those to others. The Church teaches that as all human beings are made in the image of God, they deserve fair treatment.

> Torture which uses physical or moral violence to extract confessions, punish the guilty, frighten opponents, or satisfy hatred is contrary to respect for the person and for human dignity. (*Catechism of the Catholic Church*, 2,297)

Catholic views on radicalisation

REVISED

Radicalisation is a process where a person begins to support extreme ideas (often religious ideas) associated with terrorist groups. They may reach a point where they will use indiscriminate violence and commit terrorist acts.
- The Catholic Church is against radicalisation as this increases tension, hurts the innocent and people should work, as far as possible, for respect and understanding.
- Where there is social injustice or people feel excluded from society this can make them vulnerable to being radicalised. Many people, including Catholics believe it is important to tackle social injustice.

Catholic views on martyrdom

REVISED

In a general sense, a **martyr** is anyone who suffers and dies for their faith. The word means 'witness'. In a Catholic sense, it means someone who died specially for their Catholic faith, and martyrs are remembered in prayers at the mass.

- Jesus spoke about facing suffering and death for the faith (Matthew 16:24). Martyrs are honoured for their faith and courage, standing up for their beliefs.

- Non-religious people or groups also honour anyone who is killed for abiding by their beliefs and their conscience. Protestors and campaigners for social justice can end up in this position, as seen in the cases which secular groups such as Amnesty International supports.

Catholic perspectives on conflict resolution

REVISED

- Jesus urged people to be peacemakers, describing peacemakers as blessed and sons of God (Matthew 5:9).
- St Paul urges believers to make peace with one another (2 Corinthians 13:11).
- The Church urges peace making. They believe that the task of establishing peace is a process that can involve struggle at times and that listening and understanding is needed on both sides to establish a respectful relationship.

> Peace making calls for courage, much more so than warfare. Instil in our hearts the courage to take concrete steps to achieve peace. (Pope Francis, 2014)

Examples of organisations working for peace

Pax Christi works for peace and conflict resolution. This was founded after World War II to work for reconciliation between the French and the Germans and has since become a worldwide organisation rejecting violence and getting involved in conflict resolution where possible. They held a conference on Nuclear Disarmament in 2013 and wrote to Pope Francis in 2014 before his meeting with President Obama.

Non-violent resistance

REVISED

Non-violent resistance is achieving change through non-violent means, there are many different forms for example, peaceful demonstrations, refusing to work and hunger strikes.

- Non-violent resistance is allowed by the Catholic Church. Individuals have campaigned for social justice and set up aid centres or relief movements for the poor and marginalised, such as the Catholic Dorothy Day (1897-1980) in the USA. Her work refused violent protest and conflict no used non-violent protest and examples of social justice.
- Non-violent protest has been used by other faith leaders such as the Hindu Mahatma Gandhi in India to gain independence for India between 1945 and 1948, and the Protestant pastor, Martin Luther King to gain rights for African Americans in the USA in the 1960s.
- Secular and atheistic individuals have also used peaceful protest at times against nuclear weapons (a good example was the women's camp at the missile base in Greenham Common in the 1980s) and other causes such as the policy of introducing fracking.

Now test yourself

1. While the Church condemns terrorism, the root causes must be recognised. What might some of these be?
2. What does the Catechism say about the use of torture?
3. Describe the work of Pax Christi or the Justice and Peace Commission.
4. Explain how the work of Dorothy Day was a form of non-violent protest.

TESTED

Key terms

A **Martyr** is someone who dies for their beliefs. Catholic martyrs are those who died for the Catholic faith.

Radicalisation is gradually adopting extreme and intolerant views in religions or politics.

Terrorism is violence used to create fear and force social change.

Theme C: Religion, human rights and social justice

Human rights and religious freedom

Biblical teaching about the dignity of all humans

REVISED

- Genesis 1:27 teaches that human beings are all made in the image of God and all have equal **dignity**. No one is better than or superior to another. All have the right to fair and just treatment.
- Jesus reminded people of the Old Testament command to love thy neighbour as yourself (Mark 12:31).
- St Paul reminds people of God's love for all and the need to end division in Colossians 3:11.
- Micah 6:8 hopes for peace and justice between people, which honours God. Love of neighbour is part of human dignity and love of God is impossible without it.

> **Dignity** is the worth and value of a person. In Christianity, all people are created equal in God's image.

Catholic understanding of human rights

REVISED

Human rights can be found listed by the United Nations and many different thinkers and movements. The Church bases these upon creation and the image of God, and then the Scriptures and the Tradition. The Catholic Church believes that there are a set of basic rights and freedoms that every person should have. Human rights respect the dignity that each person has because they were made in the image of God. Rights are linked to responsibilities, including the duty to protect others.

- Catholic teaching on human rights is presented in the Vatican II document, *Gaudium et Spes* 26. This states that everyone should be treated fairly and have their basic needs met, whatever their race or beliefs. 'Therefore there must be made available to all men everything necessary for leading a life truly human, such as food, clothing and shelter; the right to choose a way of life freely and to found a family…'.
- The human rights presented in *Gaudium et Spes* are very similar to those taught by Jesus in the parable of the Sheep and the Goats (Matthew 25:31–46).
- Pope Paul VI commented to the UN in 1972, 'The Church feels wounded in her own person whenever a man's rights are discarded or violated, whoever he is and whatever it is about.'

> **Human rights** are that all human beings are entitled to certain rights in their freedom and needs.
>
> **Freedom of religion** is the right to believe and practise a faith or to believe in no faith.
>
> **Common Good** is Catholic social teaching about understanding the needs of all people.

> Every day human interdependence grows more tightly drawn and spreads by degrees over the whole world . As a result the **common good**… today takes on an increasingly universal complexion and consequently involves rights and duties with respect to the whole human race. (*Gaudium et Spes* 26)
>
> The social order requires constant improvement. It must be founded on truth, built on justice and animated by love. (*Gaudium et Spes* 26)

Catholic attitudes to freedom of religion or belief

REVISED

Article 9 of the Human Rights Act says everyone in the UK is entitled to Freedom of thought, belief and religion. **Freedom of religion** means that a person may practice any religious (or non-religious) belief they choose. While Christians in the past, Catholics included, have sometimes not respected the religious freedom of those who didn't share their faith, religious freedom and tolerance is now clearly taught by the Church:

- Vatican II document, *Dignitatis Humanae* 2, said that everyone is entitled to religious freedom and no-one should be forced to act against their beliefs: 'the human person has a right to religious freedom…no one is forced to act in a manner contrary to his own beliefs.'
- Pope Francis has called for cooperation between people of different beliefs and views: 'Believers and non-believers can work together to promote a society where injustice can be overcome…'.

How belief in human rights may be expressed in action by individuals and the Church

REVISED

Sadly, people are denied these rights in some parts of the world, and might be imprisoned for their political or religious views.

- Catholic groups such as CAFOD campaign for famine relief and health provision in the developing world.
- Aid to the Church in Need is a Catholic charity trying to raise funds to help refugees, asylum seekers and Christians persecuted for their faith.
- The L'Arche communities, set up by a Catholic lay person, Jean Vanier, enable the disabled to live together in caring communities with helpers.
- Christian Aid is an ecumenical charity working to combat poverty, illiteracy and famine in the developing world.
- Non-religious groups such as Amnesty International work to help prisoners of conscience, persecuted for their political opinions or their race and not only for their religion.

Now test yourself

TESTED

1 What does Genesis 1:27 teach about the image of God?
2 List the human rights found in *Gaudium et Spes*.
3 What did Pope Francis say about people with other religious beliefs?
4 Name one Catholic and one non-religious group who work for human rights. Say what they do.

Theme C: Religion, human rights and social justice

Perspectives on wealth

Catholic teachings on wealth

- The Catholic Church is particularly concerned for the most vulnerable and marginalised members of society.
- The Bible does not say that everyone should be poor, though some are called to give up material goods such as monks, friars and nuns. Others might be called to be missionaries and work in very poor areas. Most people need to live peacefully and use their material goods wisely to raise their families and to support society.
- The parable of the talents (Matthew 25:14–30) shows that some will have more riches than others, but the important thing is how they are used. With wealth comes responsibility to use it fairly and wisely and not to become selfish or to exploit the poor.
- The Catholic Church has spoken out against the poverty of some in the world and the unjust distribution of wealth. *Gaudium et spes* 63 states: 'While an immense mass of people still lack the absolute necessities of life, some, even in less advanced countries, live sumptuously or squander wealth.'

Catholic teachings on stewardship of wealth

- **Stewardship** of wealth means handling wealth responsibly. It means ensuring a fair distribution of money and using money to provide opportunities for employment and growth, rather than using it to buy riches for a few at the expense of others.
- The example of Joseph in the Old Testament is cited as wise stewardship as he ordered surplus grain to be stored for when there was a famine (Genesis 41).
- Pope Francis has spoken about the need for stewardship of wealth, appealing for solidarity, standing with others and not ignoring them. 'It presumes the creation of a new mindset which thinks in terms of community and the priority of the life of all over the appropriation of goods by a few.' (*Evangelium gaudium* 188)

> **Stewardship** is the need to be responsible with material goods, and to care for the environment.

Catholic teaching about wealth creation

- The Catholic Church is not against wealth creation. There needs to be enough for all for the wellbeing of society and individual human rights.
- They believe that wealth should not just be accumulated for the few but should be used to help the whole of society.
- The parable of the rich man and Lazarus (Luke 16:19–31) is an example of the unfair distribution and use of wealth.

Greed, materialism and the value of individuals

- St Paul taught that the love of money is the root of all evil.
- Jesus, in the Sermon on the Mount, taught that charity to those who have little was important. The Sermon on the Mount also says, 'Blessed are the poor, for theirs is the kingdom of God.' Individuals are worth more than their material wealth or lack of it.
- Saints have often given up their material comfort for love of others such as St Francis of Assisi.
- Ecumenical Christian groups such as Christian Aid try to redistribute wealth to the needy in the developing world.
- Non-religious groups seek to help those in need, not being offended by their poverty, such as the homeless charity Shelter, or the Big Issue with its vendors.

Catholic teaching about exploitation of the poor

Exploitation of the poor means treating poor people unfairly in order to make money. It happens when people put the accumulation of wealth first, above the needs of others. The poor can be exploited in many ways:

- making them work long hours for very low wages
- employing children
- making them work in very poor or unsafe conditions.

The Catholic Church teaches:

- The prophet Amos spoke out against the exploitation of the poor (Amos 8:4–7).
- The exploitation of the poor is denounced by the Church as it is an abuse of people's rights, and all people are made in the image of God, have equal dignity and should be respected. Catholic charitable organisations such as CAFOD work around the world helping the poor and vulnerable.

Human trafficking

Human **trafficking** is when people are sold into slavery or made to work as prostitutes. They have often been promised jobs or homes, but are then exploited.

- The Catholic Church condemns this as a betrayal of human rights and justice, and works with agencies to help such people.

- The Bakhita Foundation in the UK was set up to help people caught up in human trafficking. This is named after an African young woman, Bakhita, who was sold into slavery but escaped and eventually became a nun and then made a saint.
- Voices in Exile helps to support and advise asylum seekers in the UK, based in large cities. In Brighton, for example, they have community meals and advice sessions with health workers and lawyers.

> **Trafficking** is the movement of vulnerable refugees and selling them into slavery or forcing them to work as prostitutes.

The wealth of the Church

REVISED

The Catholic Church is one of the wealthiest organisations in the world and some people say it is hypocritical for the Church to be so wealthy when it says that wealth should be shared and used for the good of everyone. However, the Church would argue:

- Much of its wealth is made up of the buildings it owns and these are being used for the good of society, providing education, health care and religious services. The Church also needs wealth to run and maintain these services.
- Pope Paul VI sold the ornate and expensive triple crown that Popes used to wear and the money was given for aid in developing nations. He wished to act in charity and also showed humility.

- Since Pope John XXIII some of the Vatican works of art have been sold to give money to international aid.

> Any Church community, if it thinks it can comfortably go its own way without creative concern and effective cooperation in helping the poor to live with dignity and reaching out to everyone, will also risk breaking down, however much it may talk about social issues or criticise governments. (Pope Francis, *Evangelii Gaudium* 207)
>
> Everyone should be able to draw from work the means of providing for his life and that of his family, and of serving the human community. (Catechism of the Catholic Church, 2,428)

Now test yourself

TESTED

1 Explain what is meant by stewardship.
2 What ideas about wealth can be found in the parable of the talents?
3 What is human trafficking and what attitude does the Church have to this?
4 Give two ways in which the Church is not as wealthy as some suggest.

Perspectives on poverty

Christian duty to act against poverty

REVISED

Poverty means when income is below a certain level. Some people live in absolute poverty which means that they don't have enough money to meet their basic needs. Others live in relative poverty which means they are poor in comparison to the rest of the society they live in.

The Catholic Church teaches that individuals and communities have a responsibility to help those who are poor and to tackle the causes of poverty. They believe that people living in poverty cannot live in the full dignity they should have because they are made in the image of God, so Catholics should help to combat poverty.

> **Preferential option for the poor** is the Catholic teaching that the needs of the poorest must come first.

The preferential option for the poor

- The **preferential option for the poor** means that the needs of the poorest people should be put first in terms of aid, financial help, medical help and education.
- Catholics believe that in the same way Christ died to benefit all of humanity, Catholics should also think about others not just themselves.
- Pope Francis talked about serving the needs of the poor in Evangelii Gaudium. He said that Catholics should look after the poor and also that poor people are closer to Jesus than rich people because they are suffering like he did.
- Aiding the poor is the virtue of compassion. Compassion means literally 'suffering with' another or others. To have compassion means to come alongside those in need.

> This is why I want a Church which is poor and for the poor. [...] We are called to find Christ in them, to lend our voice to their causes , but also to be their friends, to listen to them, to speak for them and to embrace the mysterious wisdom which God wishes to share with us through them. (*Evangelii Gaudium*, 198)

Christian views on action against poverty

REVISED

- Christians believe that they have a responsibility to look after others in the Christian community as well others outside the Church.
- The Church teaches that love has to be shown in actions: words and prayers are not enough. Catholics must actively work to tackle poverty.
- The parable of the Good Samaritan (Luke 10:25–37) is a reminder of this from the teaching of Jesus. Our neighbour is anyone in need and not just someone of our race or faith.

> If a brother or sister is naked and lacks daily food, and one of you says to them, 'Go in peace; keep warm and eat your fill', and yet you do not supply their bodily needs, what is the good of that? So faith by itself, if it has no works, is dead. (James 2:15–17)

How should the poor be helped?

- In the Catholic Church, there are charitable groups such as the St Vincent de Paul Society (SVP) that supports the infirm in the parish and gives financial aid to those in need. A branch of this is De Paul which helps the homeless.
- A non-Catholic Christian group is Tearfund which raises awareness of the Developing world and raises funds. Street Pastors is another example as a series of trained helpers walk the streets of cities at night giving counsel and practical support, particularly for the homeless, addicts and drunks.
- However, giving people money is not the solution to poverty. The reasons for poverty also need to be faced. Otherwise people will always rely on aid and never be able to support themselves.
- So some people argue that rather than giving money to the poor it is better to use it to provide tools or employment opportunities so

that the poor can begin to build their own livelihoods. The Fairtrade organisation does this by ensuring farmers are paid fair wages and sells products that have come from these workers.

- Another way to tackle poverty would be to campaign against some of the causes of poverty, for example the Make Poverty History campaign aimed to cancel some of the debts owed by poor countries to rich ones.
- Some people also feel that just giving money to those in poverty means that they won't try and get out of poverty themselves.
- Some people feel that some of those in poverty are responsible, or partly responsible themselves, such as drug addicts or alcoholics, who often can become homeless. They would argue that they should help themselves. However, the question also has to be asked why they got into these difficulties in the first place. Was there enough support in place for them?

Christian action

REVISED

We have seen that Christians believe that they have a duty to help the poor and show them compassion. Charities such as CAFOD or Christian Aid put these values in to action by helping with financial, food and medical aid. Individual people can donate money to support these organisations.

CAFOD

CAFOD is a Catholic Charity that works for international development. It works with the Bishops of England and Wales, and partners with many groups and projects abroad.

- CAFOD works with particular local projects rather than development in general, whether medical or to do with famine or clean water. E.g. sanitising poor sewerage systems helps to prevent diseases like diarrhoea and typhoid.
- CAFOD campaigns for justice, and put pressure on the UK government to honour its legal responsibilities by paying out 0.7% of its income on overseas aid.

Christian Aid

Christian Aid is a Christian charity that aims to bring an end to poverty around the world.

- Christian Aid works especially with climate change (which affects farmers in developing countries).
- Christian Aid works on gender issues such as helping prevent female genital mutilation (FGM).
- Christian Aid works against diseases such the prevention of AIDS and malaria in developing countries.

Other secular agencies and campaigns work to eradicate poverty and to help with specific projects, such as Comic Relief and Live Aid.

Now test yourself

TESTED

1 Explain what is meant by the 'preferential option for the poor'.
2 What does James 2:15–17 teach about attitudes to poverty?
3 What are street pastors, and how do they help those in need?
4 Give three ways in which Christian Aid acts against poverty.

Prejudice and discrimination

Racial prejudice and discrimination

REVISED

Racial **prejudice** is having negative ideas about a person based only on their race or culture.

Racial **discrimination** is acting in a certain way because of the ideas you hold about someone based on race.

Being prejudiced and discriminating against people on the basis of their race is called racism. Discrimination on the basis of race is illegal in Britain but every year there are still many instances of racism. After the decision for Britain to leave the EU, many Eastern Europeans living in Britain received racist abuse.

> **Prejudice** is prejudging sometime, not having possession of all the facts.
>
> **Discrimination** is acting out of prejudice to stop people having access to places or jobs.

Christian teaching on racial prejudice and discrimination

REVISED

- Catholics believe a person should not be judged by the colour of their skin or their race, but upon the fact that they are a human being, made in the image of God. Pope Francis commented that such prejudice and discrimination also hurts the one doing it as it demeans them.
- All Christians oppose racial prejudice and discrimination, or should do, if they follow the teachings of Christ. There have been times when this has not been the case, such as the acceptance of slavery by the Catholic Church, the Anglican Church and others. The Dutch Reformed Church in South Africa used to teach that the black Africans were inferior to the whites. It was Biblical principles that helped to change these attitudes.
- Non-religious groups often oppose racism such as Humanists and the UN Declaration on Human Rights is accepted by many faiths and also non-religious groups.

> Whatever insults human dignity poisons human society, but do more harm to those who practise them than those who suffer the injury. (Pope Francis, *Evangelii Vitae* 34)

Catholic teachings about equality and justice

REVISED

Equality

Catholics believe that all people are equal because:
- human beings are all made in the image of God (Genesis 1:27)
- Christ died for everyone, regardless of gender or race
- St Peter was challenged to share the Gospel with non-Jews as well as Jews (Acts 10:34).

Justice

The command to 'love your neighbour as yourself' is at the heart of Catholic teaching about justice. It means fairness to all. Catholics believe that every person should be treated fairly as every person is made in God's image and is equal in dignity.

> Social justice comes about where the inalienable dignity of every person is respected and the resulting rights are safeguarded and championed. (YouCat 329)

Promoting tolerance and racial equality

Catholics have a duty to put the values of equality and justice in to action. Examples of ways they help promote tolerance and racial equality are:

● Catholic schools are open to various ethnic groups, including some non-Catholics and also non-Christian faiths, such as Muslims. This helps to create mutual respect.

Supporting victims of racial prejudice

● The Catholic Church has many ethnic groups within its schools, as mentioned above, including the children of refugees who have fled terrible conditions of war, persecution or famine. The schools have a responsibility to educate and support these children and, indirectly, their families. They will have been subjected to discrimination and abuse because of their race or faith.

● The work of groups such as the SVP can aid refugee families of ethnic origin. They will give a listening ear and help with money, food and second-hand furniture from their depots.

Attitudes to gender and sexuality within religion

REVISED

Gender

● Catholic teaching stresses the equality of men and women, but also their differences. Catholics believe that men and women are equal but different.

● The Catholic Church believes that the work women have traditionally done raising children and running the home should be highly valued, but also supports women who want to (or have to) work outside the home.

● However, only men can be priests in the Catholic Church. This is because the twelve disciples were all male, and priesthood is seen as a sacrament and not a job, so the Catholic Church does not view this as gender discrimination. The Catholic and the Orthodox Churches only therefore ordain men, whereas the Anglican Church allows women to be ordained.

● Some people may see the Catholic and Eastern Orthodox insistence on an all-male priesthood as gender discrimination. However, men and women are still distinct. Sacraments depend in part on their symbolic power. For example, the priest at the altar reminds us of Jesus at the table of the Last Supper. He was male, and the teaching of the Church respects this, meaning that for the priest to be an accurate image the celebrant should be male.

Sexuality

● Homosexual people should be respected as human beings and not discriminated against or subjected to hate speech.

● Homosexual sex is prohibited as sex is understood as belonging to married men and women. Catholics believe that sex should be procreative (open to resulting in children), and homosexual sex cannot do this.

● The Church asks those who experience same-sex attraction to live a chaste life, strengthened by the grace of the sacraments and the encouragement of friends who share the same values.

> Homosexuals must be accepted with respect, compassion and sensitivity. Every sign of unjust discrimination in their regard should be avoided. (Catechism of the Catholic Church, 2,358)

Now test yourself

TESTED

1 What is the difference between racial prejudice and racial discrimination?
2 What did Pope John Paul II say that the effect of racism is on individuals?
3 Give one example of how the Church tries to help victims of racial discrimination and abuse.
4 How would the Church answer the charge that they are prejudiced and discriminate against women and against homosexuals?

Theme D: St Mark's Gospel – the life of Jesus

The early ministry of Jesus

Background

REVISED

The authorship of St Mark's Gospel is not known for certain. Mark could have been an eyewitness. Alternatively, an early tradition states, 'Mark became Peter's interpreter, and wrote accurately what [Peter] remembered.' (Papias)

John the Baptist's preparation for Jesus' ministry (Mark 1:1–8)

REVISED

- John might have been part of a movement at the time in which some Jewish people were hoping for the Messiah and were trying to purify Judaism, such as the Qumran community.
- Some of these reforming Jewish movements practiced a form of **baptism** as a ritual bath to show **repentance**. Christian baptism is understood by Catholics as something more; it is a sacrament that gives a cleansing from sin, the gift of the Holy Spirit and entrance into the Church family.
- John acted as a lone voice and promised the imminent arrival of the Messiah.
- John's dress echoed that of the Old Testament prophet Elijah (cf 2 Kings 1·8) Elijah was expected before the coming of the Messiah (cf Malachi 4:5–6).
- John's preaching contained a quote from Isaiah 40:3 about preparing a way, and also one from Malachi 3:1 about the messenger.
- The promise of the coming of the Holy Spirit was significant for the Holy Spirit was believed to have been inactive in Israel since the last of the prophets, Malachi. The Spirit would return to action with the coming of the Messiah.

> **Baptism** is an immersion in water as a sign of repentance and forgiveness for first century Jews, and a sacrament for Catholic Christians.
>
> **Repentance** is saying sorry for your sins, and turning away from what is wrong.

Jesus' baptism and temptation (Mark 1:9–13)

REVISED

- The baptism has the coming of the Holy Spirit as promised by John, and the heavenly voice speaks a message from Scripture, using part of Psalm 2:7 which was thought to have been used at the coronation of a Jewish king. There is also a reference to Isaiah 42:1 and the 'Servant of God in whom God is well pleased.'
- Christians see a hint of the belief in the Trinity here. The Father's voice is heard, the Son is present and the Spirit descends.
- The wilderness is a hint of the Exodus story when the Hebrews spent a time in the wilderness before entering the promised land. Jesus is soon to begin his ministry.

The paralysed man (Mark 2:1–12)

REVISED

- The man is brought to Jesus and lowered through the roof. The friends who brought him had faith, but he might not have. This shows that people can help and pray for others.
- Jesus' healing of the man demonstrated that he could forgive sins. Some conditions can be caused by guilt and are psychological. If this was so here, then Jesus forgiving the man freed him to walk again.
- Jesus refers to himself as the Son of Man, a title that could just mean 'a man' or could be the Messianic title of a coming deliverer (Daniel 7:13).

Jairus' daughter (Mark 5:21–24a, 35–43)

- Only Peter, James and John are with Jesus when this **miracle** is performed though the rest of **the twelve** are with him for much of his ministry.
- Jairus was one of the rulers of the **synagogue**, the local Jewish place of worship. Though Jesus was often in conflict with such people, but this man had no doubt seen or heard of his healing miracles at Capernaum and elsewhere.
- When Jesus said that the girl was only sleeping, he either meant that she was dead but not for long, or that she was in a coma and had not actually died.
- Jesus removes the mourners as they were probably professional mourners who would weep and wail for effect. He wanted genuine bereaved people

and quiet. Mark uses an Aramaic term here, '*talitha qum*' meaning literally, 'Little lamb, get up.'
- Jesus shows his authority yet again, and the instruction for the family to tell no one is another example of the Messianic secret.

> A **miracle** is either a wonderful event that helps someone or a supernatural event. Healings in the Gospels could be either, if there is a psychological root.
>
> The **twelve** means the twelve disciples
>
> **Synagogue** means 'assembly'; it is the Jewish place of gathering for prayer and worship.

The rejection at Nazareth (Mark 6:1–6)

- Jesus bemuses and disturbs people he knew well in Nazareth, his home village.
- Synagogue worship involves unrolling the scrolls of the **Torah,** the law of Moses.
- The people think Jesus' teaching is a scandal, literally 'a stumbling block' for they cannot accept the teaching and wonder where he got such a message or authority.
- Mention is made of the family of Jesus. His brothers and sisters are known, and four brothers are named. The Catholic tradition, following ancient

understandings, sees these either as cousins or more likely step-brothers. The term for brother and sister in Hebrew had a variety of meanings.
- Interestingly, Mark says that Jesus could not perform any miracles there owing to their lack of faith. Faith is necessary then for openness to God's presence and power.

> The **Torah** is the law of Moses, the first five books of the Old Testament.

The feeding of the five thousand (Mark 6:30–44)

- This is the first of two miraculous feeding miracles in Mark. He also has one in 8:1–10.
- The miracle echoes the Old Testament story in 2 Kings 4:42 where Elijah feeds 100 men with loaves. Mark is making a point that Jesus is like Elijah.
- Interpretations of this miracle vary. Either it was a nature miracle where loaves and fish were multiplied, or it was a miracle of the conversion of the human heart. The Catholic Church would always stress that Jesus could work nature miracles, however this is interpreted.
- Jesus broke the bread and shared it, as at the Last Supper. Jesus giving out food like this suggested **Holy Communion** to some.

> **Holy Communion** is the sharing of consecrated break and wine in the Eucharist.

Now test yourself

1 How was John the Baptist linked with Elijah, and why?
2 What aspects of the story of the baptism of Jesus suggest the Holy Trinity?
3 Give two possible interpretations for the miracle of the feeding of the five thousand.

TESTED

Theme D: St Mark's Gospel – the life of Jesus

The later ministry of Jesus

The conversation at Caesarea Philippi (Mark 8:27–33)   `REVISED`

- Peter was open about Jesus as the Messiah. Others were saying he was Elijah or one of the prophets, showing that they believed he was special.
- Jesus gives a **passion prediction**; a prophecy that he was to be crucified and raised up again.
- This is a turning point in the Gospel, after Jesus is clearly shown to be the Messiah. Jesus focuses on the twelve and not the crowds, beginning his journey to Jerusalem and the cross.

> **Passion prediction** is a prediction that Jesus would be rejected, crucified and then be resurrected.

The transfiguration of Jesus (Mark 9:2–9)   `REVISED`

- The transfiguration reveals Jesus as the Messiah and there is the beginning of a suggestion of divinity. Jesus was totally transfigured and shining with light, suggesting that the presence of God was fully with him.
- The light and the cloud suggests an Old Testament idea, the *Shekinah*, the presence of God (Exodus 34:29–35).
- The presence of Moses and Elijah signified the Law and the Prophets from the Old Testament, standing beside the Messiah who fulfilled them both.
- Many Christians today celebrate the Transfiguration on 6 August.

Jesus' passion prediction (Mark 10:32–34)   `REVISED`

- The disciples are following Jesus to Jerusalem reluctantly. Jesus does not calm them but warns them. He will be handed over, crucified and in three days rise up. This is the third prediction of the passion in Mark.
- In this prediction he mentions the **Gentiles**, meaning the Romans. They would not have been threatened by his religious teaching but by his threat to their power as the Messiah.
- The three days is a recurring theme in the Old Testament. Jonah was in the belly of the whale for three days, for example.
- The title Son of Man is used again of the heavenly deliverer.

> **Gentile** means a non-Jew.

The request of James and John (Mark 10:35–45)   `REVISED`

- Jesus challenges them about accepting martyrdom as he will do – the cup and the baptism are symbols of this. They say that they will, but he rebukes them for it is only the Father who can decide such things.
- The real rebuke is that the way of **Christ** is the way of a servant, not grasping after power: 'For the Son of Man himself did not come to be served but to serve, and to give his life as a ransom for many.' (10:45)
- He uses 'Son of Man' again and the frequency of this title in this Gospel might be because it was open to interpretation, and Jesus would have put his own intention into this, but keeping his Messianic identity hidden for now as the authorities would have arrested him immediately.
- '**Ransom**' means 'cover over'. Jesus was saying that his death would be for all but the exact doctrine of how this saves people is left open.
- Christians today might have many different **vocations** to serve people and the Church.

> **Ransom** is a payment paid to release someone from a duty or prison or slavery or being a hostage.
>
> **Vocation** is a call to serve others in some way.
>
> **Christ** means 'messiah', the anointed and coming king.

Bartimaeus (Mark 10:46–52)

REVISED

- Though blind, Bartimaeus could 'see' that Jesus was the Messiah more than the crowd. His reaction in Mark is like the first disciples who recognised who Jesus was and followed him.
- The story has blind Bartimaeus calling Jesus '**Son of David**'. It could have been for this reason that people tried to keep him quiet, for this was a clear Messianic title, a reference to the king. The other reason was that people thought he was pestering Jesus.
- Jesus is also called 'rabbuni', 'my **rabbi**' or 'Teacher'. Thus he is recognised as a valid Jewish teacher.
- Jesus says that Bartimaeus' faith has saved (same word as 'healed' in Greek) him. This echoes the frustration of not being able to heal in Nazareth because of their lack of faith. Faith might be a conduit here, an opening, for God's presence to work. It is not meant to be mind over matter, or inner psychic powers, though. Christ here is clearly the one who heals.

> **Rabbi** means a Jewish teacher.
>
> **Son of David** is a Messianic title as it was a king in David's line.

The entry into Jerusalem (Mark 11:1–11)

REVISED

- Jesus enters Jerusalem on a colt (a donkey or horse less than four years old). This fulfilled a prophecy in Zechariah. This describes of a humble Messiah rather than a warrior king riding on a war horse. Zechariah 14:4 says that Jesus' starting point, the Mount of Olives, was a significant place.
- The people put their cloaks in front of him, a gesture of honour and obedience, akin to a red carpet today. The palm branches would be waved in victory processions and placed on the road in front of the king. 'Hosanna' means 'save us, we pray'. The whole scene was full of Messianic imagery for those who understood. The Romans might not have done, but the Temple authorities did.
- This was nearly Passover time and Jerusalem would be filling up with pilgrims making the Romans cautious and nervous of an uprising.
- This is known as the **triumphal entry** today. This is celebrated by Christians on Palm Sunday, the Sunday before Easter Sunday when palm crosses are carried.

> See, now, your king comes to you; he is victorious, he is triumphant, humble and riding on a donkey, on a colt, the foal of a donkey. (Zechariah 9:9)

> **Triumphal entry** was Jesus' entry into Jerusalem on a donkey

Now test yourself

TESTED

1 Why were the events at Caesarea Philippi a turning point in the Gospel? Is the messianic secret employed by Mark after this?
2 How does the Transfiguration suggest Jesus' divinity, and what do Moses and Elijah represent?
3 How many predictions of the passion are there in Mark, and what Old Testament story does the three days suggest?
4 Give two details in the entry into Jerusalem that suggest that Jesus was the Messiah.

The final days in Jerusalem

The Last Supper (Mark 14:12–26)

REVISED ☐

- Mark records the Last Supper as being on the first day of the **Passover** when the Passover lamb was sacrificed in the Temple.
- Judas betrays Jesus, but his reasons for doing so are not clear. It might have been treachery and greed, for he received payment from the Jewish authorities, thirty pieces of silver, the price of a slave.
- The Eucharist is instituted as part of the Passover meal, Jesus said that now, rather than commemorating the Exodus, the meal (bread and wine) would commemorate his body and his blood.
- The words spoken by Jesus are known as the **Dominical words** ('the Lord's words') and are used in the Eucharistic prayer today. The Catholic Church believes that these words change or consecrate the elements of bread and wine into the Body and Blood.

> **Passover** is the Jewish festival which remembers the escape of the Hebrews from slavery in Egypt.
>
> **Dominical words** are the words of Jesus over bread and wine at the Last Supper.

Jesus in Gethsemane (Mark 14:32–52)

REVISED ☐

- Jesus showed fear and even prayed that he might avoid the suffering of the cross. This shows that Mark saw Jesus as fully human and knew human feelings.
- The symbol of the cup is used again here, as the fate or plan for Jesus, his lot in life.
- Jesus uses the Aramaic term '**abba**' in his prayer. This was a more intimate family term meaning 'father'.
- The kiss from Judas shows a Middle Eastern way of greeting and such a greeting of friendship only highlights the level of betrayal.
- The young man who had to run away naked might have been Mark himself. If this is so, such a detail says that this Gospel is based on some eyewitness testimony.

> **Abba** is the Aramaic for father.

The trial before the Jewish authorities (Mark 14: 53, 57–65)

REVISED ☐

- Jesus remained silent, as the suffering servant in Isaiah 53.
- The High Priest asked him a direct question – if he was the Messiah – which he should not have done under Jewish law, for the accused should not condemn himself.
- Jesus answered, 'I am' and spoke of the coming Son of Man. It was not **blasphemy** to call yourself the Messiah, but 'I am' could be seen as the divine name revealed to Moses (Exodus 3:4) or 'YHWH' in Hebrew.
- The Sanhedrin passed the death sentence which would have been death by stoning but as they had no authority to carry this out, they had to present him to the Romans for trial.

> **Blasphemy** means an offence against God and religion.

The trial before Pilate (Mark 15:1–15)

REVISED ☐

- Pilate was governor of Judea from 26–37 CE. Jewish historians of the time describe him as inflexible and cruel, having no mercy or regard for Jewish rules and beliefs.
- Pilate could see no fault in Jesus. He asked if Jesus was a king, which would have meant something dangerously political at the time. Jesus simply answered, 'You say so.' Jesus appeared to be evasive and noncommittal.

- Barabbas was a rebel who had been involved in a recent uprising.
- Pilate could have let Jesus go free, but did not. He was the man who condemned Jesus, finally.

The crucifixion and burial (Mark 15:21–47) REVISED

- As Jesus was **crucified**, he had a sign above his head, *Ieus Nazarenes Rex Iudaeorum* (Latin for 'Jesus Christ, King of the Jews.') This is often shown in artwork as INRI.
- Jesus was offered sour wine mixed with drugs to ease the pain, He refused. He was offered sour wine to drink soaked in a sponge, placed on a stick.
- Jesus cried out with the first verse of Psalm 22, 'My God, my God, why have you forsaken me?' The psalm was often recited by Jewish martyrs. It ended with victory though. The Hebrew for 'My God' is '**Eloi**' which some in the crowd mistook for Elijah the prophet. Elijah was believed to return one day at the Passover.
- The torn curtain in the Temple was at the entrance into the Holy of Holies, the most sacred section of the Temple which only the High Priest could enter once a year. This symbolised God's presence no longer being hidden away but open to all.
- Jesus was buried in haste as it was the day before the Sabbath when no work was allowed.

> **Crucifixion** was the Roman method of execution where criminals were nailed onto a wooden cross.
>
> **Eloi** is Hebrew for 'my God'

The empty tomb (Mark 16:1–8) REVISED

- Three of the women, Mary Magdalene, Mary, mother of James, and Salome, went to the tomb early on the Sunday to see if they could get into the tomb to prepare the body of Jesus properly out of respect.
- The tomb was sealed and would have taken a group of people to open it.
- The tomb was empty and the stone was rolled aside. The young man in white was meant to be an angel.
- Arguments against the **resurrection** might include claiming that the disciples stole the body, or the Romans or the Jewish leaders had hidden it to stop any veneration of it.
- Arguments for the resurrection include that the Romans would have risked people believing in the resurrection if the body had been hidden away.
- The resurrection is celebrated by Christians today on Easter Sunday.

> **Resurrection** is Jewish belief that the dead can rise in a transformed, immortal body.

Now test yourself TESTED

1 On what day was the Last Supper held? What new meaning did Jesus give to this meal?
2 Why did Jesus give an ambiguous reply to Pilate's question about being a king?
3 What is the meaning of the torn veil in the Temple?
4 Give one argument against the resurrection and one for it.

Significance and importance

Jesus' titles in St Mark's Gospel

REVISED

- **Son of God** – The most frequently used title of Jesus in Mark. It begins and ends the Gospel. It is there at the baptism, transfiguration and in the trial when Jesus is asked if he is the 'son of the Blessed one'. Christians today understand it to describe Jesus divinity, and being part of the Holy Trinity.
- **Son of Man** – This could mean 'human being' as in Ezekiel but in Daniel 7:13 it is about a heavenly figure who brings the kingdom of God. When Jesus used the title it would have been open to interpretation. Christians today understand it to describe the humanity of Jesus, one who was fully human and fully God.
- Christ (**Messiah**) – This referred to the Jewish kings of old. It means 'anointed one' and true kings were anointed with holy oil at their coronation. At the time of the Romans the Jews had no king, and many hoped for a king who would rise up and drive the Romans out, as a warrior. Thus 'Messiah' meant the coming king. The Romans would have seen this as a direct challenge. Christians today understand it to mean that Jesus fulfilled the prophecies in the Old Testament and is the deliverer of humanity.
- **Son of David** – David was the greatest Old Testament king. Kings after him were known as 'Son of David'. When it was used of Jesus by Bartimaeus (Mark 10:46–52) it had a messianic meaning. It was the coming king. Christians today understand it to show an inseparable link with the Old Testament; Jesus' resurrection is seen as proof that he was the coming 'Son of David'.

> **Son of God** is originally a royal and Messianic title, as well as an extremely holy person. Later, a divine title.
>
> **Son of Man** is the heavenly man in Daniel, but later understood as the human part of Jesus.
>
> **Messiah** means anointed one, king.
>
> **Son of David** is a Messianic title, descendent of King David.

St Mark's portrayal of Jesus as teacher and miracle worker

REVISED

- Jesus is as much a healer as a teacher in Mark, with story after story in the Gospel narrative. Jesus' miracles are signs of his divine power, and reveal a lot about who he is. For example, the healing miracles are evidence of Jesus' compassion and the exorcisms show that he confronted evil.
- Some Christians are happy to accept the healing miracles but not the **nature miracles**, seeing these as exaggerations or as symbolic, for example, stilling the storm is about having faith and calm in the middle of stress and persecution.
- Some Christians do not believe in Jesus' healing miracles, thinking that they could have different explanations such as that Jesus might have triggered an ability of the mind to heal the body, using faith and the Spirit of God.
- Non-religious people such as humanists would see the miracles as legends and exaggerations that were added onto the story of Jesus as time passed. Jesus is to be respected as a great moral teacher but nothing more.

> **Nature miracle** is a miracle where the normal laws of physics are set aside.

Jesus at the Last Supper

REVISED

- Catholics, Orthodox and some Anglican Christians believe that the bread and the wine used in the Eucharist, based upon the Lord's Supper, change into the body and blood of Christ. This is known as transubstantiation in the Catholic tradition, and generally as 'the real presence'.

- In the Catholic tradition, the dominical words lead to transubstantiation. In the Orthodox tradition the Holy Spirit coming upon the bread and wine lead to it.
- Protestants see the Eucharist, or Holy Communion service, as symbolic of the body and blood of Christ. They do not actually change, and the real presence of Christ is within the heart of the believer and with the gathered community ('Where two or three are gathered in my name, there I am with them.' Matthew 18:20)

Death, resurrection and empty tomb

REVISED

- The death of Jesus was a cruel execution of an innocent and holy man. All people see that, including people of no faith and other faiths. Christians see it as something more, as God's action to redeem the world. There are different ideas of how this was achieved:
  1 A sacrifice to **atone** for sin, like the biggest and best sacrifice possible.
  2 A victory over death and the devil for Jesus did not stay dead.
  3 A way of showing that God is involved in the suffering of the world and leads people through and beyond it.
  4 An act of sacrificial love for the world, as he forgave those who were tormenting him.
  5 A confirmation of the truth of his divinity.
- Christians believe in the resurrection. The Catholic teaching is that the body and soul of Jesus rose, the flesh and blood being transformed into a spiritual body that would never die again. The tomb was therefore left empty.
- Some more liberal Christians struggle with the physical body rising and the empty tomb, believing only in the spiritual raising of Jesus.
- Humanists, agnostics and atheists tend to see it as legend or as a symbol of good triumphing over evil.

> **Atone** means to make up for, cover, wash away.
>
> **Transubstantiation** is, in the mass, the invisible reality or substance of the bread and wine change into the Body and the Blood of Christ, but the external, visible forms remain those of bread and wine.

The authority of St Mark's Gospel

REVISED

- Mark is seen as the earliest Gospel, but some question how much of it was written by John Mark, the disciple who is mentioned in Acts 12:25. He accompanied St Paul and Barnabas on their missionary journeys. His mother, Mary, used her home as a meeting place for the early Christians.
- If not, then the Gospel is an early collection of narratives, teaching and miracles that emerged from the early Christian community.
- It is thought that the Passion narrative would have been the earliest section of this, used in worship.
- This early collection was thought authoritative enough to form the core of St Matthew and St Luke's Gospels, whoever actually wrote it.
- Many of the original eyewitnesses would still have been alive when St Mark's Gospel was written.

Now test yourself

TESTED

1 What is meant by the terms 'Son of God' and 'Son of Man'?
2 What is meant by the terms 'Christ' and 'Son of David'?
3 What are the two types of healing miracle? Give one explanation of either type that some people try to suggest.
4 Give any two of the four ways that Christians have of explaining how the death of Jesus brought salvation.

Theme E: St Mark's Gospel as a source of spiritual truth

The Kingdom of God

Parable of the sower (Mark 4:1–9, 14–20)

REVISED

- The Kingdom of God means the rule of God, a spiritual way to live under his rule, and the peace that will come from that. Jesus often used parables about this as it is a difficult concept. His **parables** taught that it began within the individual.
- A parable can sometimes have different levels of meaning or interpretations, but these are to the point.
- The parable of the sower has the sower as the preacher, the seed as the Word of God, and the different types of ground represent different types of people and their responses:
  1 Seed on the path – people who do not listen to the Word, Satan takes it away from them.
  2 Seed on the rocks – people who begin to respond but soon give up when life gets difficult.
  3 Seed in thorns – people who are too interested in material things and ignore the spiritual.
  4 Seed on good soil – people who hear and receive the Word properly.
- The parable of the sower is thus an **allegory** of the call to discipleship.

> A **parable** is a made up story with a spiritual truth.
>
> **Allegory** is when ordinary, material details are used in a story to suggest spiritual truths.

Parable of the growing seed (Mark 4:26–29)

REVISED

- This short parable is only found in Mark. It is addressed to the disciples as it is not involved in a debate with others.
- The kingdom is the seed this time, and it grows in a quiet and hidden manner within people. People have to be patient.
- This might have been said against the Zealots who wanted violent revolution.
- Jesus warned that judgement would come one day. The image of the harvest is used for this in the Bible (cf Joel 3:13).
- This parable is relevant today for Christians facing persecution in different parts of the world. They feel particularly threatened in Iraq with extreme Muslim groups and militia. Some are driven out of their homes and become refugees, others lose their lives. However, there are moving examples of local communities supporting them as good neighbours, and even helping them to rebuild ruined churches.

Parable of the mustard seed (Mark 4:30–32)

REVISED

- The mustard seed is very small and grows into a bush large enough for birds to nest in. It grows without human effort.
- The kingdom grows slowly but surely as people respond to the Word of God.

- The reference to the birds suggests Gentiles being invited into the kingdom along with Jews. Daniel 4:10-12 has the image of a tree that provides food for all.
- Building the kingdom today can be found in groups such as CAFOD and Christian Aid and wherever love is shown for people who are suffering.

Parable of Jesus and the children (Mark 10:13–16)

- The kingdom was to be received like a child, with trust, innocence and humility.
- The saying, 'Let the little children come to me […]' is used by Christians today to welcome children into worship, and to have various activities for them. Catholics, Orthodox, Anglicans and some other Christians are all baptised as infants who cannot speak for themselves.

Parable of the rich man (Mark 10:17–27)

- The rich man was following the Law, the Torah, as best as he could. This was called **halakah**, meaning to walk in the way of the Law and the teaching of the rabbis.
- He did not see any connection between riches and halakah. Perhaps he even thought that earthly riches were a sign of blessing.
- Jesus challenged him to follow him. The man could not, and was like the seed that fell among the thorns in the parable of the sower.
- The eye of the needle was a striking and ridiculous image about how hard it was to be a rich and a disciple. Some think this was a reference to a narrow gate in Jerusalem, but others now doubt this.
- Christians today are not against wealth but the way this is handled, and the attitude to it. Having wealth can also be a blessing to others that you help.

> **Halakah** means to walk in the way of the Torah

The greatest commandment (Mark 12:28–34)

- Jesus was asked four questions to test him in Mark 12.
- Jesus used two scriptures to answer this, rather than one commandment. The **Shema** from Deuteronomy 6:4 is about God being one and only he should be worshipped. The love of neighbour verse is from Leviticus 19:18.
- The questioner agreed that justice to others was more important than rituals and sacrifices. This was close to the attitude of Jesus who followed the 8th century BCE prophets who condemned the people for their rituals when they were acting unjustly (cf Amos 5:21–24).
- Christians today are to reject all forms of racism as all human beings are the neighbour, and this follows the parable of the good samaritan (Luke 10:29).

> **Shema** is the main confession of faith made by Jews. The Lord is one.

Now test yourself

1 Identify the four types of seed in the parable of the sower and explain their spiritual meaning.
2 Two other parables use the image of a seed. Identify these parables and sum up their message in a sentence each.
3 What is meant by halakah and why did Jesus think the rich man was not practising this perfectly?
4 What did Jesus say is the greatest commandment?

Jesus' relationships with those disregarded by society

The man with leprosy (Mark 1:40–45)

REVISED

- Certain illnesses in the ancient world were seen as God's judgement for sin. The leper might not have had what is called leprosy today but it would have been an awful skin disease that would have made him cast out of normal society, living outside the city and begging.
- Such people would be seen as unclean spiritually. No one was supposed to touch them.
- Jesus reached out in compassion and touched him.
- Jesus asked him to keep quiet, and this is an aspect of Mark's Messianic secret again.
- Christian missions have worked with lepers, such as Father Damien in the Catholic Church and the Leprosy Mission.

The call of Levi (Mark 2:13–17)

REVISED

- **Tax collectors** were hated members of society at the time. They were Jews who worked for the Romans and could charge extra money if they wished for their own profit. Thus they were seen as traitors.
- Jesus entered Levi's house, which would have been a scandal for a religious teacher to do. He ate with him, which in the Middle East is seen as a gesture of acceptance.
- The Pharisees rebuked him for eating with tax collectors and sinners but Jesus responded that he had come to call sinners, as a physician cures the sick.
- Christians today operate many charities that help those on the fringes of society, helping with homeless projects such as Emmaus (started by a Catholic priest, Abbé Pierre, in France after World War II).

> **Tax collectors** were Jews who collected taxes for the Romans and charged extra.

The Syro-Phoenician woman's daughter (Mark 7:24–30)

REVISED

- Jesus and the disciples had entered Tyre which was **gentile** territory.
- The Syro-Phoenician woman begged Jesus to heal her daughter. News of his authority and healing miracles were now spreading beyond Jewish communities.
- Jesus refused at first, saying that the children are to be fed first before food is given to the dogs. (The children here are the Jews, the dogs the pagans.)
- Jesus was concerned at this point to minister to the Jews only before the Gospel was to go out to all the world. He did not mean to insult the gentile woman.
- Jesus listened as she did not give up, rather like blind Bartimaeus. He showed mercy and heals the child, saying that the dogs can at least catch the crumbs that fall from the table.
- Jesus praised the woman's faith, noting that this was greater than what he found among many of the Jews.
- Christians today oppose racism and **discrimination** based on race or gender. After the resurrection, the Apostles went out into all the world.

> **Gentile** means a non-Jewish person.
>
> **Discrimination** is actions that are based upon prejudice and that target different ethnic groups, beliefs or gender.

The demon-possessed boy (Mark 9:14-29)

REVISED

- This story involves an **exorcism** of an evil spirit. Reading the text today it sounds as though the boy was epileptic, severely so, having grand mal seizures. At that time, illnesses like this would be seen as the work of the evil spirits, which is now rejected. The Church would remind people today that evil forces can exist, though.
- Jesus spoke to God as 'Abba', an Aramaic term for 'Father' and this closeness to God would be possible for Christians after the resurrection and gift of the Holy Spirit.
- Modern day Christians can hold healing services where hands are laid on people for healing, and in Catholic churches, they might receive the sacrament of the sick, also. **Shrines** attract many **pilgrims** who sometimes claim that they have been healed through prayer, such as Lourdes in France.

> **Exorcism** means to free people from an evil spirit.
>
> A **shrine** is a special place and church where a Saint is buried or the Virgin Mary is said to have appeared.
>
> A **pilgrim** is someone who journeys to a holy place to pray.

The widow at the treasury (Mark 12:41–44)

REVISED

- Widows were vulnerable in the ancient world. They were protected within Judaism (this was a religious duty) but were often poor.
- The widow dropped only two small coins into the treasury plate, while many others were donating large sums of money, being rich.
- The offerings were checked by the priests and then announced – the giving was not private. The widow's two coins were lepta, the smallest coins available. When her offering was announced, she would have been easily mocked.
- Jesus praised the woman for giving what little she had. Discipleship can often involve giving something up.
- Charities depend upon donations today, such as OXFAM and CAFOD. Parish churches also depend upon offerings from the worshippers or they could not function.

The anointing at Bethany (Mark 14:1–9)

REVISED

- The **anointing** took place two days before the Passover.
- Simon the leper had obviously been healed by Jesus and was hosting the disciples.
- A woman anointed Jesus over his head with expensive perfume of nard. Anointing could happen for coronations of monarchs (Jesus is seen here as the Messiah) and also of bodies for burial. There is a twofold meaning here, of kingship and preparation for burial.
- Mark does not name the person who criticised her, claiming that the perfume was too expensive and the money should not have been wasted (other Gospels suggest it was Judas Iscariot). Jesus praised her faith and recognised the symbolism of the action.
- 'You always have the poor with you' is used as an inspiration to support charities today. It does not mean that anyone should be poor and efforts should be taken to remedy this.

> **Anointing** means to pour oil over the head.

Now test yourself

TESTED

1 Why was it surprising for Jesus to meet and help a leper? How did this story show the Messianic Secret?
2 Why would the call of Levi have been scandalous at the time?
3 Why did Jesus not help the Syrian-Phoenician woman at first, and what did he say about her afterwards?
4 What are the two meanings that can be found in the incident of anointing Jesus' feet?

Faith and discipleship

The call of the first disciples (Mark 1:16–20)

- The first **disciples** were fishermen on the Sea of Galilee.
- The **call** of Andrew, Simon, James and John was without discussion. They immediately left their nets and belongings to follow Jesus.
- A disciple is a 'learner' or 'follower'. These men were not promised anything apart from getting converts.
- Some Christians today are called by God to give up everything they have such as monks or nuns. Others are called to do certain things but not to leave everything behind. Discipleship always involves commitment.

> A **call** is a sense of a vocation, a path to follow or a task to undertake. In religious terms, it is a call to follow the gospel in some way.
>
> **Disciple** means literally a 'learner' or student, and often seen as a follower of a teacher.

The woman with the haemorrhage (Mark 5:24b–34)

- The woman in this story had a flow of blood, a **haemorrhage**, which would have classed her as unclean, she could not be touched or enter the Temple.
- Jesus was not concerned that she had touched his clothes, just as he was not afraid to touch a leper.
- She was frustrated with the doctors of her time that they could not cure her. She had heard of Jesus' healing miracles and reached out through the crowd, like Bartimaeus.
- Jesus was able to heal without knowing that anyone was there; 'power had gone forth from him'.
- Jesus told her to go in peace ('**shalom**') and called her daughter, a term that showed he viewed her with respect.
- Though Christians today have much faith in medical science to treat them, they are also open to spiritual healing through prayer and the laying on of hands.

> **Haemorrhage** means continuous bleeding that can be life-threatening.
>
> **Shalom** is Hebrew for 'peace', inner stillness and the absence of war.

The mission of the Twelve (Mark 6:7–13)

- The twelve were sent out on mission by Jesus, trained for when they would have to go out and spread the Gospel.
- They were told to:
  1 Carry a staff – this showed they would have to walk far and defend themselves if need be.
  2 Take no bread, money or bag – they were to rely on faith and the gifts of others.
  3 Wear sandals and take one shirt – they were to travel simply, sandals being needed for stony paths.
  4 Stay in the same house where they were welcomed – they were safe there and should bless the house.
  5 Wipe the dust from their feet – they had to leave behind anyone who rejected them and move on.
- The disciples preached that people should turn from their sins (repentance); they freed people from evil spirits and they cured the sick.
- Christians today are involved in mission in many ways. Some go out as missionaries, teaching and performing works of mercy, running orphanages, schools or hospitals, for example. Others support Christian charities. All **Christians** are to help others where they can in the name of Christ.

The costs and rewards of discipleship

REVISED

- Jesus spoke of the cost of discipleship. People would not always listen, understand or be peaceful.
- The call to take up the cross and follow Jesus was radical for its time. It was disturbing and a reference to Jesus' crucifixion to come. Discipleship could mean suffering and not only giving things up.
- The reward of discipleship was eternal life.
- This would have encouraged the early Christians who suffered for their faith in the Roman Empire.
- Jesus promised the disciples that those who had given up so much for the kingdom of God would receive blessings in this world and in the next.
- This shows different values from the world, and hope for lower classes and those on the fringes of society.

Peter's denials

REVISED

- Jesus had warned the disciples that many would fall away, and Peter would deny him three times before dawn ('when the cock crows').
- Peter had followed to watch what happened at the house of the high priest. A servant girl recognised Peter and his Galilean accent.
- He denied knowing Jesus, and repeated this twice until the cock crowed. He was distraught and wept.
- Peter denied knowing Jesus out of fear or arrest and suffering, and perhaps also anger and confusion that Jesus did not resist arrest as the Messiah.
- For Christians today, many lessons can be learned from this passage.
  1 Peter had courage and then panicked; many Christians today can struggle with their faith.
  2 Peter's tears showed that repentance is possible.
  3 Peter's error shows that even an important leader of the Church is not perfect.
  4 After repenting, Peter did great, bold work for the Gospel.

> **Ascension** is when Jesus returned to heaven forty days after the resurrection.
>
> **Commission** is when the risen Jesus gave a future mission to the Eleven disciples.

The commission and ascension

REVISED

- The disciples received their commission at the final encounter with the risen Jesus;
  1 They were to preach to all the world.
  2 Believers were to be baptised and judgement would one day come.
  3 Believers would heal by the laying on of hands, drive out demons, speak in other tongues (cf Acts 2:1–12) and be empowered by the Holy Spirit.
  4 Picking up snakes and drinking deadly poison were probably symbolic of being safe from danger.
- The **Ascension** of Jesus was about his authority over creation, taking his seat at the right hand of the Father (the place of honour). This showed he was the Messiah, as he had predicted this during his trial.
- Christians today have the commission to work for the Gospel in actions and in words in many ways. The early Christians spread out from the Holy Land into the Roman Empire and North Africa. The Catholic Church is engaged in worldwide mission with evangelistic missions and charities such as CAFOD.

Now test yourself

1 Which disciples were called first, and what message did Jesus give to them?
2 What instructions did Jesus give to the disciples when he sent them out, and why were they to do this?
3 How many times did Peter deny knowing Jesus, and what inspiration can this story give to modern day Christians?
4 What did the story of the Ascension suggest for the first disciples?

TESTED

Significance and importance

The kingdom of God

REVISED

- The kingdom of God is understood as something present in the world as people work to spread the Gospel and change things. Changes that bring peace and justice are part of the spread of the kingdom.
- The kingdom is something future when Jesus returns.
- The kingdom is something within people, their forgiveness, their hope, the gift of the Holy Spirit.
- The kingdom can be found in the Christian communities that love and worship together, including many different ethnic backgrounds and social groups.

First century attitudes

REVISED

- Lepers and women with any flow of blood such as a haemorrhage were excluded from religious rituals and many aspects of society as they were considered unclean.
- Tax collectors were seen as traitors as they were Jews who worked for the Romans.
- Gentiles were seen as outsiders as they did not worship the one God, often being polytheistic and not following the Torah.
- Samaritans were outsiders as they belonged to an ancient breakaway group from Judaism.

Jesus' attitudes

REVISED

- Jesus touched and healed lepers, he allowed the woman with the haemorrhage to touch his clothes, and he healed the child of a Gentile woman.
- Jesus shows inclusivity to different groups and needy people. Christians today should follow this example and not reject or exclude anyone because they are different or poor or ill.

Jesus' disciples

REVISED

- Disciples, then and now, can face challenges such as mockery and indifference, or even arrest and martyrdom. In the West, the challenges are usually indifference and mockery as secular society can have little time for faith. It is often caricatured as simplistic and primitive.

Faith

- The faith of the man who was paralysed healed him, the faith of Jairus helped his daughter to live, the faith of the Syrophoenician women healed her child. The disciples were rebuked for losing faith during the storm, and Peter for denying Jesus.
- For modern Christians, faith is essential to help them believe and trust, often when people around them do not.

Authority and Jesus' teaching

- Jesus teaches with authority in Mark such as with the incident of the man lowered through the roof, or the man with the withered hand, or the teaching in Nazareth. This authority was spiritual and derived from his status as God and man.
- Christians can seek this authority today when they faithfully follow his teachings and repent of their wrongdoing. They can be striking witnesses to an unbelieving society. Actions also have authority when the poor are fed, the homeless sheltered or peace is made between groups.
- Secular authority denies the spiritual and is materialistic, side lining faith. It is often relativist, recognising many different competing views, except that the physical world is the only reality that there is.

Now test yourself

1 Explain the three ways of understanding the coming of the Kingdom of God.
2 Which groups were excluded from the Kingdom of God according to Jewish thought of the time?
3 Give one example of how Jesus showed that socially excluded people were to be included in the Kingdom of God.
4 Give one example of how Jesus teaching with authority surprised the scribes and the Pharisees.

Theme E: St Mark's Gospel as a source of spiritual truth

Exam practice: Judaism - beliefs

1 What is meant by chesed?
  A Justice
  B Charity
  C Loving kindness
  D Repairing the world [1]

2 Which of the following means 'the world to come'?
  A Tikkun Olam
  B Gehenna
  C Gan Eden
  D Olam ba-ha [1]

3 Name two Prophets God made covenants with. [2]

4 Name two types of mitzvot. [2]

5 Give two reason Jews believe Tikkun Olam is important. [2]

6 Explain two ways in which a belief in the Law influences Jews today. [4]

7 Explain two ways in which a belief in 'loving kindness' influences Jews today. [4]

8 Contrast the beliefs of Judaism and the main religious tradition of Great Britain about the Messiah. Refer to two differences in your answer. [4]

9 Contrast the beliefs of Judaism and the main religious tradition of Great Britain about God. Refer to two differences in your answer. [4]

10 Explain two Jewish teachings about Shechinah (The Divine Presence). Refer to scripture or another source of Jewish belief and teaching in your answer. [5]

11 Explain two Jewish beliefs about God as Law-giver and judge. Refer to scripture or another source of Jewish belief and teachings in your answer. [5]

12 Explain two Jewish teachings about the importance of the Covenants. Refer to scripture or another source of Jewish belief and teaching in your answer. [5]

13 'Mitzvot between man and God should the most important mitzvot for Jews today.' Evaluate this statement. In your answer you should:
  ● refer to Judaism
  ● give reasoned arguments in support of this statement
  ● give reasoned arguments to support a different point of view
  ● refer to the teaching of Judaism
  ● reach a justified conclusion. [12]

14 'Life here and now is more important than the afterlife for Jews today.' Evaluate this statement. In your answer you should:
  ● refer to Judaism
  ● give reasoned arguments in support of this statement
  ● give reasoned arguments to support a different point of view
  ● refer to the teaching of Judaism
  ● reach a justified conclusion [12]

15 'It is impossible to repair the world, so the Messianic Age will never happen.' Evaluate this statement. In your answer you should:
  ● refer to Judaism
  ● give reasoned arguments in support of this statement
  ● give reasoned arguments to support a different point of view
  ● refer to the teaching of Judaism
  ● reach a justified conclusion [12]

ONLINE

Commentary

Grade 2 candidates have a weak knowledge of how to show the similarities within a faith. Questions asking about these are very difficult. If this is you – make some notes about two similarities for each element, and then learn them.

Grade 5 candidates can point out similarities within the faith, although their answers will lack depth. It is often the case they know 'some', so the exam can be very testing – if it doesn't fit what they know. If this is you, then you need to do more work on learning these aspects.

Grade 8 candidates know about a religion in depth. They can write easily and clearly about similarities within the faith, as they know how to present these without just repeating themselves.

Exam practice: Judaism - practices

1 What is meant by kosher?
  A   Lawful
  B   Forbidden
  C   Blessing
  D   Legal document for marriage   [1]
2 Which of the following is the Oral Law?
  A   Torah
  B   Tefillin
  C   Talmud
  D   Tenakh   [1]
3 Give two rules about milk and meat.   [2]
4 Give two things that Jews do on the Friday Shabbat.   [2]
5 Name two prayers used by Jews.   [2]
6 Explain two ways in which beliefs about kashrut influence Jewish diet.   [4]
7 Explain two contrasting ways in which a boy's Bar Mitzvah and a girl's Bat Mitzvah are carried out   [4]
8 Explain two contrasting features of a Jewish wedding in two Jewish traditions.   [4]
9 Explain two ways in which beliefs about Shabbat influence Jewish life.   [4]
10 Explain two ways in which Shabbat is important in the life of a Jew. Refer to **scripture or another source of Jewish belief and teaching** in your answer.   [5]
11 Explain two purposes of the marriage ceremony in Judaism. Refer to **scripture or another source of Jewish belief and teaching** in your answer.   [5]
12 Explain two ways in which prayer is important for Jews. Refer to **scripture or another source of Jewish belief and teaching** in your answer.   [5]
13 'Jewish mourning is more about supporting the living than remembering the dead.' Evaluate this statement. In your answer you should:
  ● refer to Judaism
  ● give reasoned arguments in support of this statement
  ● give reasoned arguments to support a different point of view
  ● refer to the teaching of Judaism
  ● reach a justified conclusion.   [12]
14 'Pesach is more important than Rosh Hashanah.' Evaluate this statement. In your answer you should:
  ● refer to Judaism
  ● give reasoned arguments in support of this statement
  ● give reasoned arguments to support a different point of view
  ● refer to the teaching of Judaism
  ● reach a justified conclusion.   [12]
15 'Rites of passage in Judaism are outdated.' Evaluate this statement. In your answer you should:
  ● refer to Judaism
  ● give reasoned arguments in support of this statement
  ● give reasoned arguments to support a different point of view
  ● refer to the teaching of Judaism
  ● reach a justified conclusion.   [12]

ONLINE

Commentary

Grade 2 candidates use simple language, and simple sentences. They generally make mistakes in spellings. If this is you, try using more connectives, and take more care with spellings.

Grade 5 candidates use a mix of simple and complex sentences. Their use of connectives can be limited (and repetitive!). If this is you, become more consistent in writing better sentences, and find a range of connectives – so you aren't always using the same (boring!) three!

Grade 8 candidates use complex language and sentences – they sound very impressive!

Exam practice: Religion, relationships and families

1 Religious believers disagree with sexism. What type of prejudice is sexism?
   A Against race   C Against gender
   B Against colour   D Against age   [1]

2 Many religions forbid cohabitation. What is cohabitation?
   A Living together as an unmarried couple   C An extended family living together
   B Living together when married   D Living with parents   [1]

3 Give two Catholic ideas about family planning.   [2]

4 Give two of the marriage vows.   [2]

5 Give two reasons why Christians choose to have children.   [2]

6 Explain two contrasting beliefs in contemporary society about the rights of same-sex couples
   to have children.
   ● You must refer to Christian belief.
   ● You must refer to contrasting religious and/or non-religious belief.   [4]

7 Explain two similar beliefs about the use of contraception.
   ● You must refer to Christian belief.
   ● You must refer to contrasting religious and/or non-religious belief.   [4]

8 Explain two similar beliefs about the inequality of men and women.
   ● You must refer to Christian belief.
   ● You must refer to contrasting religious and/or non-religious belief.   [4]

9 Explain two Christian beliefs about adultery. Refer to **scripture or another source of
   Christian belief and teaching** in your answer.   [5]

10 Explain two Christian beliefs about humans as sexual beings. Refer to **scripture or another
   source of Christian belief and teaching** in your answer.   [5]

11 Explain two Christian beliefs about the purpose of the family. Refer to **scripture or another
   source of Christian belief and teaching** in your answer.   [5]

12 'The vows are the most important symbol of a marriage ceremony.' Evaluate this statement.
   In your answer you:
   ● should give reasoned arguments in support   ● should refer to Christian arguments
     of this statement   ● may refer to non-religious arguments
   ● should give reasoned arguments to support   ● should reach a justified conclusion.   [12]
     a different point of view

13 'It is wrong to divorce.' Evaluate this statement. In your answer you:
   ● should give reasoned arguments in support   ● should refer to Christian arguments
     of this statement   ● may refer to non-religious arguments
   ● should give reasoned arguments to support   ● should reach a justified conclusion.   [12]
     a different point of view

14 'Adoption should not be restricted to married couples.' Evaluate this statement. In your answer you:
   ● should give reasoned arguments in support   ● should refer to Christian arguments
     of this statement   ● may refer to non-religious arguments
   ● should give reasoned arguments to support   ● should reach a justified conclusion.   [12]
     a different point of view

ONLINE

Commentary

Grade 2 candidates give unsupported opinions in answers to evaluation questions. This means they often only give their own ideas on something, and rarely give two sides. If this is you, try to think of and present an alternate view to your own.

Grade 5 candidates give more than one side in evaluation answers, however, often do not focus closely enough on the statement. So reasoning is loose, and limited. If this is you, underline key words/phrases in the statement and always check back to it with each argument you write.

Grade 8 candidates give more than one side, focus clearly on the statement, and develop their reasoning with good detail.

Exam practice: Religion, peace and conflict

1 Many religious believers disagree with WMDs. What does WMD stand for?
   A   Weapons of mass devastation   C   Weapons of mass destruction
   B   Nuclear weapons   D   Weapons of mass death   [1]

2 Religious believers disagree with repeated behaviour designed to hurt someone emotionally or physically. What is the term used for this?
   A   Friendship breakdown   C   Assaull
   B   Bullying   D   Unkindness   [1]

3 Give two rules from the Just War Theory.   [2]

4 Give two reasons a religious person might forgive their persecutor.   [2]

5 Give two ways a religious believer can help victims of war.   [2]

6 Explain two contrasting beliefs in contemporary British society to WMDs.
   ● You must refer to Christian belief.
   ● You must refer to contrasting religious and/or non-religious belief.   [4]

7 Explain two similar beliefs about martyrdom.
   ● You must refer to Christian belief.
   ● You must refer to contrasting religious and/or non-religious belief.   [4]

8 Explain two similar beliefs about violent protest as a response to injustices.
   ● You must refer to Christian belief.
   ● You must refer to contrasting religious and/or non-religious belief.   [4]

9 Explain two Christian beliefs about forgiveness. Refer to **scripture or another source of Christian belief and teaching** in your answer.   [5]

10 Explain two Christian beliefs about justice. Refer to **scripture or another source of Christian belief and teaching** in your answer.   [5]

11 Explain two Christian beliefs about terrorism. Refer to **scripture or another source of Christian belief and teaching** in your answer.   [5]

12 'For a Catholic, violence can never be justified.' Evaluate this statement. In your answer you:
   ● should give reasoned arguments in support   ● should refer to Christian arguments
     of this statement   ● may refer to non-religious arguments
   ● should give reasoned arguments to support   ● should reach a justified conclusion.   [12]
     a different point of view

13 'Catholics should be at the forefront of peace-making activities in the modern world.' Evaluate this statement. In your answer you:
   ● should give reasoned arguments in support   ● should refer to Christian arguments
     of this statement   ● may refer to non-religious arguments
   ● should give reasoned arguments to support   ● should reach a justified conclusion.   [12]
     a different point of view

14 'A Christian should always forgive wrongs done to them.' Evaluate this statement. In your answer you:
   ● should give reasoned arguments in support   ● should refer to Christian arguments
     of this statement   ● may refer to non-religious arguments
   ● should give reasoned arguments to support   ● should reach a justified conclusion.   [12]
     a different point of view

ONLINE

Commentary

Grade 2 candidates often struggle with key terms, which mean they miss questions out – simply not knowing what they are being asked. If this is you, you start by learning the key words.

Grade 5 candidates usually know the key terms, but understanding can be limited. This means answers are often limited. If this is you, you need to work on knowing more detail (e.g. relevant teachings).

Grade 8 candidates know the key terms and use them fluently and well, making the examiner see their clear understanding.

Exam practice: Religion, human rights and social justice

1 What is meant by 'stewardship of wealth?
   A Handling wealth responsibly
   B Saving money
   C Giving to charity
   D Investing money   [1]

2 Religious believers 'do not agree with the exploitation of the poor'. Which of these would not be seen as exploitation of the poor?
   A Excessive loans
   B Minimum wage
   C Making people work in unsafe conditions
   D Making people work for long hours for very low wages   [1]

3 Give two ways Christians can follow the command to 'love your neighbour'.   [2]

4 Give two reasons why Christians disagree with people trafficking.   [2]

5 Give two teachings from the 'Preferential Option for the Poor'.   [2]

6 Explain two contrasting beliefs in contemporary British society about racial discrimination.
   ● You must refer to Christian belief.
   ● You must refer to contrasting religious and/or non-religious belief.   [4]

7 Explain two similar beliefs about the use of wealth.
   ● You must refer to Christian belief.
   ● You must refer to contrasting religious and/or non-religious belief.   [4]

8 Explain two similar beliefs about the dignity of all humans.
   ● You must refer to Christian belief.
   ● You must refer to contrasting religious and/or non-religious belief.   [4]

9 Explain two Christian beliefs about wealth creation. Refer to **scripture or another source of Christian belief and teaching** in your answer.   [5]

10 Explain two Christian beliefs about action against poverty. Refer to **scripture or another source of Christian belief and teaching** in your answer.   [5]

11 Explain two Christian beliefs about equality. Refer to **scripture or another source of Christian belief and teaching** in your answer.   [5]

12 'Religious believers should not be rich.' Evaluate this statement. In your answer you:
   ● should give reasoned arguments in support of this statement
   ● should give reasoned arguments to support a different point of view
   ● should refer to Christian arguments
   ● may refer to non-religious arguments
   ● should reach a justified conclusion.   [12]

13 'Religious believers do not show enough compassion in the world.' Evaluate this statement. In your answer you:
   ● should give reasoned arguments in support of this statement
   ● should give reasoned arguments to support a different point of view
   ● should refer to Christian arguments
   ● may refer to non-religious arguments
   ● should reach a justified conclusion.   [12]

14 'There is never an acceptable reason to discriminate.' Evaluate this statement. In your answer you:
   ● should give reasoned arguments in support of this statement
   ● should give reasoned arguments to support a different point of view
   ● should refer to Christian arguments
   ● may refer to non-religious arguments
   ● should reach a justified conclusion.   [12]

ONLINE

Commentary

Grade 2 candidates don't make it easy for the examiner to give marks. Their writing can be confused, too brief, and too vague. If this is you, you just need to learn the content better – start by making notes which work for you.

Grade 5 candidates use a mix of clear and vague ideas. Often the examiner has to look for where new ideas start. If this is you, try giving more clues – a new idea means a new paragraph, and you say 'Firstly..' and 'Secondly...' before your points.

Grade 8 candidates write clearly and use clear signals for the examiner to work with.

1 Which name is Hebrew for 'God is saviour'?

  A Moses   C Jesus

  B David   D John   [1]

2 By whom was Jesus baptised?

  A Moses   C John

  B Joseph   D David   [1]

3 Give the names of two of Jesus' disciples. [2]

4 Give two miracles performed by Jesus. [2]

5 Give two titles Mark uses for Jesus in his Gospel. [2]

6 Explain two contrasting views about the authorship of St Mark's Gospel. In your answer you must:
- refer to Christian views.
- refer to contrasting religious or non-religious views. [4]

7 Explain two contrasting views in contemporary British society about the empty tomb. In your answer you must:
- refer to Christian views
- refer to contrasting religious or non-religious views. [4]

8 Explain two similar views about Jesus' actions at the Last Supper. In your answer you must:
- refer to Christian views
- refer to contrasting religious or non-religious views. [4]

9 Explain two ways in which Jesus shows his power. Refer to St Mark's Gospel in your answer. [5]

10 Explain two ways in which the title 'Son of Man' is important in St Mark's Gospel. Refer to St Mark's Gospel in your answer. [5]

11 Explain two ways in which Jesus is portrayed as a teacher in St Mark's Gospel. Refer to St Mark's Gospel in your answer. [5]

12 'The most important event in St Mark's Gospel was the baptism of Jesus.' Evaluate this statement. In your answer you should:
- give developed arguments to support this statement
- give developed arguments to support a different point of view
- refer to St Mark's Gospel
- reach a justified conclusion. [12]

13 'Mark was more interested in what Jesus did than who he was.' Evaluate this statement. In your answer you should:
- give developed arguments to support this statement
- give developed arguments to support a different point of view
- refer to St Mark's Gospel
- reach a justified conclusion. [12]

14 'St Mark's Gospel has no relevance in the 21st Century.' Evaluate this statement. In your answer you should:
- give developed arguments to support this statement
- give developed arguments to support a different point of view
- refer to St Mark's Gospel
- reach a justified conclusion. [12]

ONLINE

Commentary

Grade 2 candidates show little knowledge of the diversity within or between religions. If this is you, you need to get notes which are better for you to work with.

Grade 5 candidates show some knowledge of diversity and an understanding of how this influences different people – but it is often only the most obvious ideas, and then understood in a superficial way. If this is you, focus your notes and revision on specific groups within religions so you can write clearly and knowledgably.

Grade 8 candidates show good knowledge and understanding of the diversity within and between religions. They demonstrate this clearly in detailed answers.

Exam practice: St Mark's Gospel as a source of spiritual truth

1 In the Parable of the Sower how many types of soil did seed fall on?

A 2   C 4

B 3   D 5   [1]

2 Levi was a disciple of Jesus. What was his job?

A Doctor   C Tax collector

B Farmer   D Fisherman   [1]

3 Give two parables told by Jesus.   [2]

4 Give two of Jesus' disciples.   [2]

5 Give two reasons Christians see discipleship as important.   [2]

6 Explain two contrasting views about discipleship. In your answer you must:
   ● refer to Christian views
   ● refer to contrasting religious or non-religious views.   [4]

7 Explain two contrasting views about the Kingdom of God. In your answer you must:
   ● refer to Christian views
   ● refer to contrasting religious or non-religious views.   [4]

8 Explain two different views about the importance of faith. In your answer you must:
   ● refer to Christian views.
   ● refer to contrasting religious or non-religious views.   [4]

9 Explain two ways that Jesus showed care for the disregarded in society. Refer to St Mark's Gospel in your answer.   [5]

10 Explain two teachings about the Kingdom of God in St Mark's Gospel. Refer to St Mark's Gospel in your answer.   [5]

11 Explain two ways that Peter's denials were important. Refer to St Mark's Gospel in your answer. [5]

12 'Christians in the 21st century should base their faith on the greatest commandment.' Evaluate this statement. In your answer you should:
   ● give developed arguments to support this statement
   ● give developed arguments to support a different point of view
   ● refer to St Mark's Gospel
   ● reach a justified conclusion.   [12]

13 'Faith is more important than action in St Mark's Gospel.' Evaluate this statement. In your answer you should:
   ● give developed arguments to support this statement
   ● give developed arguments to support a different point of view
   ● refer to St Mark's Gospel
   ● reach a justified conclusion.   [12]

14 'The Kingdom of God is a personal mind state.' Evaluate this statement. In your answer you should:
   ● give developed arguments to support this statement
   ● give developed arguments to support a different point of view
   ● refer to St Mark's Gospel
   ● reach a justified conclusion.   [12]

ONLINE

Commentary

Grade 2 candidates don't know the different stories within St Mark's Gospel, they confuse the parables, they don't know what happened in what order, nor the significance of any. If this is you, you need to go back to basics – get your notes sorted into a timeline for example, make a series of numbered revision cards and find something which helps you remember the individual stories (a picture, perhaps).

Grade 5 candidates have a good overview, but the detail isn't there. They might confuse things – e.g. what is the difference between the Parables of the Mustard Seed and the Seed?! They might know some well, and others not so – bad news if the second types are on the exam! If this is you, making your revision notes a little more memorable will help.

Grade 8 candidates know St Mark's Gospel well, and can answer correctly each time. They don't mix up similar stories and they do know the importance of them all.

Now test yourself answers

1 Creation

Forms of expression

1 God is pictured as high above the world and in a cloud.

2 Adam is touched by God, showing that he is in the image of God and has a unique dignity in creation.

3 The painting uses light and an abstract image of God having no shape.

4 In Michelangelo's *The Creation of Adam*, God is a human figure. In Elizabeth Wang's *Heart of God*, God is not a human-type figure, but a shining light.

Beliefs and teachings

1 God is beyond the universe, beyond the creation as Creator.

2 Adam received the breath of life directly and the animals were named by him.

3 The command was to look after the earth and care for it as the dominant species.

4 There is free will; stewardship of the earth; the dignity of human beings and the sanctity of life.

Sources of authority

1 The Scriptures were transmitted orally, then written down by scribes and the different books were collected by the Church.

2 The types of writing are laws; stories; history; sayings; prayers; poems and songs of praise.

3 The parts of the New Testament are the Gospels; the Acts; the Epistles and Revelation.

4 The sanctity of life means the protection of life from conception to death, and the cherishing of it as special and God's gift.

5 No contradiction is seen between science and faith because science investigates the creation, and God is the Creator beyond the universe.

Practices

1 Leviticus 19:18 says that people must love their neighbours as themselves.

2 The Greatest Commandment is to love God with all your heart and your neighbour as yourself.

3 Environment and neighbour are related as life on earth is interconnected, and hurting nature and resources will harm others.

4 Sustainability, as practiced by CAFOD, tries to respect and look after the earth's resources.

2 Incarnation

Forms of expression

1 Ichthus stands for 'Jesus Christ, Son of God, Saviour'.

2 The Alpha and Omega symbols show Catholic belief that Jesus is God incarnate as he is the beginning and the end, God beyond time.

3 The Sacred Heart image symbolises Christ's love which, through his suffering on the cross, lasts forever (burning with passion). Some Christians find this gruesome as the heart is exposed.

4 The crucifix reminds people of the suffering of Jesus on the cross. Some Christians object to this as they feel that it does not convey the resurrection: that fails to show that Jesus did not stay dead.

Beliefs and teachings

1 John's Gospel opens by teaching that Jesus is the Word of God made flesh.

2 Son of God can mean the king, but also a holy man in whom the fullest revelation of God is found. For Catholics, it also means the Second Person of the Holy Trinity.

3 Son of Man means a human being and is also the title of a heavenly deliverer.

4 Jesus shows his humanity by eating, drinking and weeping when Lazarus died.

5 Jesus is shown to be divine by the virgin birth, his miracles, the resurrection and the ascension.

Sources of authority

1 The Beatitudes are nine sayings of Jesus that open the Sermon on the Mount. Each of them starts with 'Blessed are …'

2 St Irenaeus of Lyons stated that Jesus was with the Father from the beginning, as the Word, and teaches humanity about God.

3 Jesus fulfils the Law as God incarnate and as the perfect man.

4 Jesus practices the virtues by helping the poor, the weak and the sick.

5 Pope Benedict XVI said that Jesus made the Word of God visible on earth.

Practices

1 Grace is the free gift of God's undeserved love.

2 Sacraments are efficacious signs, and they perform what they symbolise.

3 The Seven Sacraments are baptism; Eucharist; confirmation; confession; anointing of the sick; marriage and holy orders.

4 The matter of confirmation is the oil of chrism and the form is the gift of the Holy Spirit.

5 Catholics oppose abortion because human beings are in the image of God, the weak and innocent are to be protected; and human life develops gradually from the zygote into a baby.

3 The triune God

Forms of expression

1 Music tries to express deep feelings about God that cannot be put into words.

2 The types of Christian music are psalms; plainchant; hymns and worship songs.

3 Chants and acclamations emphasise different sections of the liturgy and also signify their importance.

4 People stand for the Gospel and lit candles may be held alongside the book, as well as incense used. The 'Alleluia' chant is used before the reading.

Beliefs and teachings

1 The Holy Trinity is God the Father, Son and Holy Spirit: three Persons in one God.

2 The Trinity is seen in the baptism of Christ in the presence of the Son, the heavenly voice of the Father, and the descent of the Holy Spirit 'like a dove'.

3 To say that the Son was 'only begotten' means that he is from the Father for all time, without beginning or end.

4 Belief in the Trinity helps Catholics with mission because the Holy Trinity, within itself is sharing and loving. This teaches Catholics to be open and sharing with others, and acting in love, which can be done in mission.

Sources of authority

1 St Augustine spoke of the lover, the beloved and the love between them.

2 St Augustine saw the Persons of the Trinity having the gifts of unity, equality and harmony.

3 Emphasis should be given to God's action in the world and not in his own nature. The Persons are seen at work in the Father sending, the Son restoring and the Spirit inspiring.

4 The immanent Trinity is about the inner life of God; the economic Trinity is about the external action of God within the world.

5 The Council of Nicaea stated that the Son and the Holy Spirit are of one substance with God the Father.

Practices

1 Matthew 28:19 has Jesus telling the disciples to baptise people in the name of the Father, the Son and the Holy Spirit. Water is poured three times in baptism to represent the three persons of the Holy Trinity into whose name the person is baptised.

2 Prayer can be defined as raising the mind and heart to God.

3 Postures or gestures in prayer can be kneeling or bowing; prostration; hands together or raised. These can suggest humility; surrender; devotion or praise.

4 Traditional prayers are well known and express ideas well. Spontaneous prayers help people to freely express themselves.

4 Redemption

Forms of expression

1 Some churches are cross-shaped to emphasise the death of Christ and the salvation this brings. Circular buildings emphasise unity and sharing.

2 The crucifix is a reminder of the death of Christ and the redemption Catholics believe this brings.

3 The altar is a place of sacrifice, where the body and blood of Christ are made present as the bread and wine are transformed.

4 The tabernacle is a secure container for the blessed sacrament, reserved for taking to the sick and also to pray and adore.

5 Protestants do not have an altar but a table, as they reject the belief that Christ is really present in the elements of bread and wine. The table suggests sharing the symbolic meal.

Beliefs and teachings

1 Restoration of the cosmic order is shown in the Ascension of Christ, which shows his victory and authority over the universe.

2 Grace means that God offers the gift of mercy even when it is not deserved.

3 Salvation is past (the cross), present (people co-operate with the grace of God), and future (salvation yet to be completed, but some have thought that this implies that good works are more important than the cross).

4 Protestants understand 'justification by faith' by seeing salvation as the work of Christ alone on the cross and this does not depend upon people's responses or actions.

5 The liturgy of the Eucharist shows the idea of redemption by remembering the Last Supper and the death and resurrection of Jesus.

Sources of authority

1 St Mark's account of the crucifixion teaches redemption by: the darkness around the cross being defeated, and the veil in the Temple is torn open.

2 John's account of the resurrection shows a belief in redemption by: The renewed faith of the disciples; the risen Christ and Mary Magdalene representing the New Adam and Eve; and the risen Christ showing a transformed humanity.

3 The Ascension shows future redemption by having the risen Christ taking authority over creation and being in the presence of the Father.

4 St Anselm understood redemption as a ransom from sin by the perfect man, with perfect obedience, restoring honour or making satisfaction to God for the disobedience of humanity.

5 The Catholic Church teaches that no one should go against their conscience, but they should inform their conscience. There are principles to follow such as the golden rule.

Practices

1 The mass is a sacrifice in two ways, an offering of praise and thanks, and also the offering of the body and blood of Christ which is represented on the altar, remembering the cross.

2 Mass comes from the Latin 'missio' meaning 'mission' or 'to be sent out'.

3 Catholics pray before the Blessed Sacrament to honour the presence of Christ and to strengthen their faith.

4 The Words of Institution are the Dominical Words, the words spoken by Jesus at the Last Supper; 'This is my Body. This is my Blood.'

5 Protestants see the Eucharist as a symbol and a reminder of the cross, though some Anglicans believe in the real presence of Christ.

5 The Church and the Kingdom of God

Forms of expression

1 The Stations of the Cross represent the journey of Christ to the cross. There are fourteen traditionally.

2 Pilgrimage is travelling to a holy place for prayer. Life is like a journey, as is the spiritual life.

3 Jerusalem was where Jesus died and rose again; Rome was where St Peter was martyred; Walsingham is special because of the belief in a vision of the Virgin Mary in 1061; Lourdes is a place of healing based upon St Bernadette's vision of the Virgin Mary.

4 *The Mission* and *Les Misérables* both contain the themes of mercy and forgiveness and self-sacrifice. The priests in *The Mission* also have to follow their conscience.

Beliefs and teachings

1 The Kingdom of God is the reign of God, peace and wholeness for humanity.

2 The Kingdom comes within the believer; through the cross; in the gift of the Holy Spirit; and at the end of time.

3 Catholic social teaching reminds Catholics that the Kingdom of God covers social justice and interpersonal relations as well as spiritual matters. Pope Leo XIII reminded employers that they should treat their workers justly.

4 *Dei verbum* teaches about scripture and tradition as the word of God; *Sacrosanctum concilium* reformed the liturgy and introduced the vernacular; *Gaudium et spes* is about the Church in the modern world; and *Lumen gentium* says that the Church is made up of many ministries, and the laity are part of that belonging and service along with clergy and religious.

5 *Aggiornamento* means updating. This was one of the ways Pope John XXIII described the aims of the Second Vatican Council.

Sources of authority

1 Mary is a sign of the kingdom by her perfect obedience to the message of the angel; her faith in God; following Christ right up to the foot of the cross; and in her mercy and compassion.

2 The Magnificat teaches that the poor and the humble will be blessed and that salvation includes social justice.

3 The four marks of the Church are that the Church is one, holy, catholic and apostolic.

4 Apostolic succession means the succession of bishops from the first Apostles and the teaching that comes down from them.

5 Conciliar Magisterium means the teaching of the bishops gathered together in a Council, and the Papal Magisterium is the teaching of the Pope, particularly when he speaks formally, 'ex cathedra'.

Practices

1 CAFOD works in developing countries, often partnering with local projects. DePaul helps the homeless, having been set up in 1989 and is linked with the Society of St Vincent de Paul.

2 A commitment to the religious life is a sign that shows the kingdom values of commitment and service.

3 Families are a sign that show the kingdom values of commitment and nurture in the 'domestic Church'.

4 Pope Francis has shown justice in his wearing of a metal cross rather than a gold one, as well as living a simple, humble life. He has shown peace by helping the USA and Cuba make peace in 2014–15.

6 Eschatology

Forms of expression

1 The Paschal candle suggests the light in the darkness, the alpha and omega symbol as Christ the beginning and the end, and also the five pins representing the five wounds.

2 *The Last Judgement* painting shows that death comes to all, rich or poor; judgement is shown by people being separated to the left and the right; Heaven open for the righteous; and Hell shown by souls being taken down.

3 Memorials show faith in resurrection by the term *'Requiescent in pacem'*, 'Rest in peace'. Sarcophagi show scenes from the Bible and especially the life of Christ, such as the good shepherd.

4 In care of the deceased, respecting the body and having a funeral service shows a belief in life after death.

Beliefs and teachings

1 Two ways that Jesus' resurrection gives hope for Catholics is that it is seen as triumph over death; a door opened for all to enter heaven and/or the belief in a heavenly body that all can receive.

2 St Paul uses a seed as an analogy of the physical body dying and a new life emerging.

3 Catholics believe in various aspects to eternal life. Death comes to all; Judgement comes to all; Heaven is open to all; Hell is wilful separation from God.

4 Two different Christian beliefs about judgement:

5 Judgement is seen by some Catholics as an encounter with the healing light and love of God that exposes people for who they are.

6 Two different Christian beliefs about Hell: Hell is wilful separation from God

Sources of authority

1 The parable of the rich man and Lazarus is about particular judgement, as the men are judged by Christ before the final judgement of all.

2 The parable suggests that the rich man is not in hell for he shows remorse.

3 Julian of Norwich was a fourteenth century holy woman who had a series of visions, the 'shewings' or 'Revelations'. Finally, she wrote, 'All shall be well, all manner of things shall be well.'

4 *Lumen gentium* 48 teaches that no one knows when Christ will return so believers need to be vigilant.

5 The Catechism teaches that God wills that no one should be lost and that all souls should go to Heaven.

Practices

1 The Last Rites have the three aspects of Confession, Holy Communion and anointing of the sick.

2 The Last Rites show a belief in the resurrection by the reconciliation of the dying person, the hope promised through Christ's presence in Holy Communion, and the healing promised for the soul.

3 Funeral rites encourage hope by showing a belief in resurrection; offering a mass for the departed; sprinkling with holy water as a reminder of baptism and the promise of eternal life; the Commendation of the soul to God and the angels; and the Committal at the burial or cremation where the body and soul of the departed are placed in God's hands.

4 Catholic views of the sanctity of life affect views about euthanasia in so far as life is seen as a gift and that nature should be allowed to take its course. This allows the dignity of caring for the dying and the place of final farewells.

7 Judaism – beliefs and teachings

Page 63

1 Declaration of faith in Judaism.

2 Creator; Judge; Lawgiver.

3 God created from nothing; seven days including a day of rest; days 1 to 6 were light; atmosphere; land/sea/vegetation; sun/moon/stars; fish/birds; animals/humans. It was good.

4 Laws given by God. Ten Commandments; Seven Laws of Noah/Noachide Laws.

5 Divine presence of God.

6 They can please God by serving him and following the law, so they follow the mitzvot; mitzvot govern all aspects of life, so they are always mindful of God; wear religious items, e.g. kippah; fearful of punishment.

Page 65

1 Resurrection means physically brought back to life, or reborn into a physical existence; reincarnation means same soul reborn on earth. Most Jews do not know if either is true; some Jews believe absolutely in reincarnation.

2 Olam ha-ze means life here and now; Olam ha-ba means the life to come (after death).

3 Gan Eden is a peaceful place, harmonious, good – like heaven; Gehenna is a sad place, full of torment, like hell.

4 Talmud says so; next life is unknown (whether it exists or what it is like) whereas we know this one; if we get it right in this life, then the next takes care of itself.

Page 66

1 Mashiach; the one to come; not God; anointed one.

2 Time of the Messiah; peaceful time; no hatred/ sin/intolerance; all will return to true belief.

3 Announced by Prophet Elijah; dead will rise; Messiah comes; no clear date, but God has already decided.

4 Bring political and spiritual peace to the whole world; restore Judaism as the faith of all; rebuild the temple in Jerusalem.

Page 68

1 An agreement; between Jews and God.

2 Role model for belief in God; role model for worship; considered father of faith; first true monotheist.

3 God would make of Abraham a great nation; give the Promised Land to Abraham's descendants; Abraham would be faithful; the symbol is circumcision of males.

4 An Israelite born into slavery in Egypt, but brought up in the Pharaoh's house; having fled Egypt, he was later chosen by God to free the Israelites; led them to the Promised Land; received the Ten Commandments from God.

5 Example of a man redeemed by God; brought the Law, and its interpretation; did God's bidding.

6 God freed Israelites, gave them the Promised Land; Humans to keep the Laws, keep the Sabbath holy.

Page 70

1 613 laws; *chukim* and *mishpatim*.

2 Mitzvot which are judgements such as 'Thou shall not kill'.

3 Deuteronomy; in every synagogue.

4 Actions towards God (worship) versus actions towards other people (ethics); both very important, but could be said that human:human are less selfish as helping others helps God.

5 Ability to make decisions, e.g. to follow the mitzvot or not; doing the right thing is rewarded by God.

Page 72

1 Guiding beliefs which shape the way we respond to situations.

2 Healing the world; e.g. means living in a way so as not to damage the world/waste resources.

3 Justice and charity; e.g. helping people get their human rights, helping to ease poverty.

4 Loving kindness.

5 By helping others; though *tikkun olam*; by doing things for the sake of it, not for personal gain; random acts of kindness.

6 These three principles mean a person is 'the best person' they can be – looking to be and do good, not hurting others, living in harmony with the world. Essentially these are principles common to all faiths.

Page 73

1 Belief in saving/preservation of human life, which means (saving) human life takes precedence over all other life and all other matters.

2 God made humans special; human soul is made in image of God; laws can be broken to save life; each person is made with a divinely given purpose; cannot take life.

3 Be peaceful, not violent; live by the law (protection/safety); don't take risks with life; protect life; might influence choice of job/career.

8 Judaism – Practices

Page 75

1 Synagogue.

2 A minyan (group of ten men in Orthodox/adults in Reform) is required, so they need the space for all these people.

3 Home only – circumcision, Shabbat meals, Pesach meals; synagogue only – daily services, marriage

4 Communion with God; reminds of covenant; communal aspect; key prayers said; mitzvot; etc.

Page 76

1 Aleinu, Kaddish, Amidha; Shema.

2 Three – morning, afternoon and evening.

3 Appropriate clothing (kippah/tefillin/tallit), clean, focused entirely on actions.

4 Devotion; keeps mind focused on God and keeping mitzvot; is itself a mitzvot; links Jews to history; sense of cleansing when doing this; etc.

Page 77

1 Mother prepares for Shabbat; synagogue service; candles to welcome Shabbat; family meal with rituals; Saturday – synagogue; no work; study; Havdalah.

2 Reminds of history; time to recharge; time to focus on faith; unites the family and community; etc.

3 Mitzvot and commandment; part of covenant with God.

4 Gives them a day of reflection; forces them to take a break from busy life; for many is a time to do something for others; 'Shabbos bride'; seen as top of week; etc.

Page 78

1 Torah, Nevi'im, Ketuvim – the three sets of Jewish scriptures.

2 It explains the Torah, rather than just repeat it.

3 Talmud gives Jews help in understanding the meaning behind the words and their application in daily life; provides the wisdom of the rabbis and sages through history so that they can follow the mitzvot as God wished them to. Importance shown by the respect they give it, and that they study it.

Page 79

1 Ceremony of circumcision for baby boys, held in the family home, carried out by trained person.

2 Coming of age ceremonies for boys and girls; represents the age at which a child takes their religious responsibilities on for themselves.

3 Boy is asked to read from the Torah at the Saturday service nearest his 12th birthday – he will have trained and studied to do this; he is called up to the Bimah to read before the whole congregation.

4 Traditional to commit to the faith; Judaism has been a persecuted faith, so this public commitment is important; means there is another person to make up a minyan.

Page 81

1 Under *chuppah*; recite blessings over wine, exchange rings; contract signed; speech about marriage; glass of wine shared; groom crushes glass.

2 Fulfils commandment to be fruitful and multiply; natural state for humans; blessing from God.

3 As soon as possible after death; body washed by Hevrah Kadishah and dressed in white linen; mourners' garments torn; casket carried – seven stops (NO RUSH) to grave; faces Jerusalem; prayer of mercy recited; all fill grave; bereaved pass through lines of mourners; meal provided.

4 Mourning period is *aninut* (death to burial - excused from all religious duties); shiv'ah (7 days after burial – no work, low stools, community feeds them); sheloshim (30 days after burial – some restrictions lifted); avelut (11 months – for death of parents only, recitation of prayers at synagogue); Yahrzeit candle; tzedakah; Yizkor prayer.

Page 83

1 Kosher means fit, in food what is acceptable by religious law for a Jew to eat; treyfah means forbidden, in food what a Jew may not eat according to dietary law.

2 It is a mitzvot; they always have so it is a tradition; unites the community; makes the Jews a separate people to others; shows devotion to God; means that even eating (most basic of actions) leads to thinking of God; etc.

3 Do not eat certain things, e.g. pork; do not combine certain foods – meat and milk; separate meat and milk utilities and utensils in kitchens; animals to be kosher slaughtered and blood drained.

Page 85

1 Pesach – Passover, release of Israelite slaves from Egypt; Rosh Hashanah – new year; Yom Kippur – Day of Atonement.

2 Represents the creation; days of reflection and self-improvement; the righteous gain another year.

3 Shofar – repentance; taschlich – casting of sins; honey and sweet things – hope for good year.

Commentaries on Exam Practice answers at **www.hoddereducation.co.uk/myrevisionnotes**

4 Kol Nidre service; day of fasting; synagogue services for repentance/confession.

5 Seder meal – first or second night of Pesach; follow Haggadah; leader wears kittel to celebrate freedom; three matzah, wine seder plate; extra cup for Elijah; wine drunk and drops spilled.

6 Maror means enslavement; karpas means tears of slaves; charoset means mortar made by slaves; shankbone means mighty arm of God and paschal lamb sacrifice; roasted egg means temple sacrifice.

Theme A: Religion, relationships and families

Relationships and the human condition – love and sexuality: communion and complementarity

1 Genesis 1 teaches that all human beings are equal in dignity and that men and women are created in their different identities.

2 In the Catholic Church marriage is seen as marital (i.e. faithful), unitive and procreative.

3 Two points from the Theology of the Body are that the body expresses the personality and there is a nuptial meaning of the body (the union of two sexes in marriage). (Also sin destroys marital relationships; procreation is central to the sexual union; responsible parenthood is taught to space the births of children; mutual love, dignity and respect are required between spouses.)

4 Adultery destroys the unity of marriage and breaks trust.

Perspectives on relationships – marriage, cohabitation, divorce and separation

1 To marry validly in the Catholic Church the couple needs to be free to marry; able to marry of their own free will; willing to have children; marry 'before the Church' i.e. in the presence of a Deacon or a Priest.

2 Marriage is a covenant because it is more than a contractual agreement. It is a committed relationship with mutual self-giving and respect.

3 It is the exchange of vows that actually marries you and the rings are only symbolic. The circle of the rings suggests eternity and everlasting love and commitment.

4 Annulment means that the marriage is decreed to be invalid and therefore never technically took place (though it did legally in the eyes of the State). Reasons for an annulment could include that one partner has had several affairs and has not believed in the marriage vows; they

married not of their own free will; they did not consummate the marriage (they have not had sex); they had no intention to have children; or did not understand the vows they made.

5 A divorced Catholic who remains single can receive communion.

Families and responsibilities – roles of men, women and children

1 The Church's attitude to family planning is that the birth of children can be regulated by natural family planning (NFP) which follows the natural fertility cycles of the woman's body.

2 *Humane vitae* prophesied that artificial birth control would increase promiscuity and break the unitive nature of marriage. The concern was also expressed that the State might impose limits on the birth of children.

3 The three purposes of the family are procreative, security (for the family) and educative (the parents are the first educators).

4 Men and women are different but equal in dignity and authority. They do not have set roles but if a woman wishes to be a housewife and mother that is to be honoured and protected.

5 Same-sex marriage is not acceptable in the Catholic Church because marriage is seen as the union of one man and one woman which is open to the procreation of children by their union. That is seen as the order of nature.

Gender, equality and discrimination – equality of men and women

1 Genesis 1 and 2 teaches that men and women are equal in dignity.

2 Priests can only be male in the Catholic Church as Jesus was male and they are seen as a representative of Christ at the altar. Men and women are equal but there are differences. Priesthood is a sacrament that needs a certain identity and is not just a job.

3 There is to be no discrimination between men and women in society according to the Church. Women should not be paid less for the same jobs as men, and there are no set roles, or jobs that women cannot do. They are equal in dignity, but a mother who stays at home has to be honoured in that role.

4 Gender discrimination means acting in a certain way towards someone based on your prejudice against their gender. This could include discrimination in the workplace, such as unequal pay. The church response to gender discrimination is to say that women should not be subject to gender discrimination but have the

same right to work as men. Women have the same dignity as men and should be equal in every way in secular employment.

Theme B: Religion, peace and conflict

Christian perspectives on human violence, justice, forgiveness and reconciliation

1 Jesus, in the Sermon on the Mount, roots violence in anger within people.

2 Examples of forgiveness in the New Testament are Jesus forgiving people on the cross; Jesus teaching that there can be no limit to the amount of times a person should be forgiven; Peter being forgiven after denying Christ; the 'our Father'; the parable of the unforgiving debtor.

3 Forgiveness is one sided where an individual forgives another; reconciliation is a two-way action where both parties forgive each other.

4 Jesus cleansed the temple of the money changers, overturning their tables and forcing them out. The name of the theory is the just war theory.

Christian perspectives on social justice and just war

1 The early Christians were pacifists, refusing military service.

2 Conditions of a just war include that: war is the last resort; it has a just cause; it is started by a rightful authority; it has a chance of success; it uses proportionate force; it does not harm civilians.

3 Nuclear weapons are rejected by the Catholic Church as: many innocent civilians would be killed; it would be a disproportionate response and no one could win; Pope Benedict stated that there would no victors only victims.

4 Consequences of modern warfare involve the harm done to civilians, refugees from war zones and environmental damage.

Holy war and pacifism

1 Isaiah prophesied a time when swords would be beaten into ploughs (Isaiah 2:4).

2 Pope Francis arranges meetings with different groups around the world such as Palestinians to try to work for peace. Catholic Bishops often speak out against injustices in their countries such as Eritrea. Groups such as CAFOD and Aid to the Church in Need work for reconciliation and also to help victims.

3 Pope Benedict XV issued his Peace Note in 1917 arguing for a truce and not total defeat as this

would bring more violence and retaliation in the future.

4 In *Pacem in Terris*, Pope John XXIII argued against nuclear weapons and the arms race.

Christian perspectives on terrorism and Christian initiatives in conflict resolution and peace making

1 The root causes of terrorism are issues of social injustice such as Muslim extremists resulting from oppressive governments or Western imperialism in the past.

2 Torture is seen by the Catechism as contrary to respect and dignity.

3 Pax Christi campaigns for peace and holds conferences and campaigns. The Justice and Peace Commission was set up by the Bishops of England and Wales and campaigns for justice and peace and seeks to help refugees and asylum seekers.

4 Dorothy Day rejected violent protest and held campaigns, published ideas and held demonstrations.

Theme C: Religion, human rights and social justice

Human rights and religious freedom

1 Genesis 1:27 teaches that all human beings are created equal and have dignity and rights. They are in the 'image of god' in an interior, moral and spiritual sense.

2 *Gaudium et spes* says that all people should be treated fairly regardless of their race or faith and their basic needs should be met.

3 Different groups and religions should be able to work together for a just society.

4 L'Arche supports disabled people where they live in communities with helpers (alternatively, CAFOD supports projects in the developing world.) Amnesty International is a non-religious group which supports prisoners of conscience through the world.

Perspectives on wealth

1 Stewardship is handling resources with responsibility. Joseph in the Old Testament is a good example when he stored food for times of famine. Pope Francis stated that this provided fairness and solidarity with others.

2 Some have less and some have more of skills, wealth or belongings. The parable teaches that no one should be exploited, but those with more have a greater responsibility.

3 Victims are sold into slavery or trapped in prostitution. Two Church groups that try to help such people are the Bakhita Foundation and Voices in Exile.

4 The Church has its wealth mainly in property and to a lesser extent, in art treasures in the Vatican. Pope Paul VI sold the ornate triple crown worn by the earlier Popes to give the money to charity. Pope Francis has sold some art treasures.

Perspectives on poverty

1 The preferential option for the poor puts the needs of the poorest and weakest first in society.

2 James 2:15–17 teaches that deeds are more important than words of support.

3 Street Pastors are volunteers from different Christian groups who patrol the streets at night assisting and counselling anyone who is in trouble, or drunk or needs to get medical help.

4 Christian Aid helps combat climate change; it works for gender equality and campaigns to stop FGM (female genital mutilation) and also tries to stop diseases such as malaria or AIDS.

Prejudice and discrimination

1 Racial prejudice is about having wrong ideas and feelings; racial discrimination is about wrong actions towards others.

2 Pope John Paul II taught that racism was an insult to human dignity and also harmed those who practised it as it caused a hardness of heart and immorality.

3 Victims of racial discrimination are helped by the international make up of many Catholic congregations as the Catholic Church is an international movement. Parish groups can support them in counselling and practical help. The Society of St Vincent de Paul has volunteers and resources to support refugee families and individuals with food, furniture and housing.

4 Homosexual persons are to be treated with dignity as human beings and discrimination is a sin. The controversial point for modern society is the teaching that homosexual sex is sinful, and homosexual people are asked to remain celibate.

Theme D: St Mark's Gospel – the life of Jesus

The early ministry of Jesus

1 John the Baptist dressed the same as Elijah. Elijah was expected before the coming of the Messiah according to Malachi 4:5–6.

2 The Holy Trinity is suggested in the story of the baptism of Jesus in the Father's voice, the descent of the Holy Spirit and the presence of the Son.

3 The feeding of the 5,000 can be understood as a physical miracle, i.e. the bread and fish were multiplied through prayer, or a moral miracle, where people's hearts and attitudes were changed. Then those who had brought food but hidden it began to share it.

The later ministry of Jesus

1 At Caesarea Philippi Peter stated that Jesus was the Christ and Jesus predicted the passion. The Messianic Secret was no longer used in the Gospel of Mark.

2 The divinity of Christ was shown in the Transfiguration by the presence of God, the Shekinah. Moses represented the Law and Elijah the Prophets.

3 There are three passion predictions in Mark. The three days in the tomb suggested the story of Jonah in the belly of the whale.

4 Jesus arrived on the donkey as in Zechariah 9:9, a prophecy of the coming Messiah. The people spread their cloaks and waved palms of victory, actions done at the arrival of a king.

The final days in Jerusalem

1 The Last Supper took place at the Passover. The new meaning was to switch the emphasis from the Exodus from Egypt to the person of Jesus and his sacrifice. The bread was his body, and the wine his blood.

2 Jesus avoided calling himself a king to Pilate directly as this would have been understood as a political statement when Jesus had a spiritual kingdom.

3 The tearing of the temple veil showed that the presence of God was open to the world, and that sins had been forgiven.

4 An argument against the resurrection might be that the disciples stole the body (or the Romans hid it, or that the disciples were hallucinating). The reply to this would be that the tomb was hard to open when sealed, and a Roman guard had been posted (and the Romans would have risked belief in the resurrection if they had hid the body, as people would believe that he had risen, or the disciples were prepared to die for their faith which suggests that it was more than grief and psychology).

Significance and importance

1 Son of God carried a number of meanings; a royal title, a holy person, and divinity. Son of Man suggested the heavenly man in Daniel's vision, and also a human being, the human sides of Jesus.

2 Christ meant Anointed One, or Messiah. Son of David was a Messianic title and a royal title as it meant a descendent of King David.

3 There are healing miracles and nature miracles. Some are sceptical of healing miracles saying that they are the result of belief and then mind over the body. Some see the nature miracles as symbolic, such as the water into wine. This represented the newness of the Gospel while the Old Testament was the water.

4 Jesus' death can be understood as a sacrifice for sin and a victory over evil (or as God being in the suffering of the world or an act of love and forgiveness).

Theme E: St Mark's Gospel as a source of spiritual truth

The kingdom of God

1 The four types of seed are those on the path, on the rocks, among thorns and on good soil. On the path means the Word is ignored, on the rocks means there is no depth, among thorns means that there are too many distractions, on good soil means response to the Word.

2 The parable of the growing seed suggests that the Kingdom of God grows quietly but the harvest at the end of time suggests a final point and judgement upon evil. The parable of the mustard seed also suggests that the Kingdom grows slowly and reaches completion one day.

3 Halakah means to follow the path of the Torah, the Law. The young man was too attached to his wealth.

4 To love God and your neighbour as yourself is the Greatest Commandment. This is based upon Deuteronomy 6:4 and Leviticus 19:18.

Jesus' relationships with those disregarded by society

1 Touching a leper was shocking as they were considered outcasts being under judgement because of sin. [note- author to add answer to second part of this question 'How did this story show the Messianic Secret?'

2 The call of Levi was shocking as he was a despised tax collector who were seen as traitors.

3 The woman was a Gentile and many Jews would have seen her as outside the faith. Jesus was also not ready to spread the Gospel beyond his own people of Israel. At the end, he praised her because she had shown more faith than many Jews.

4 The anointing of the feet showed that Jesus was the Messiah as kings were anointed, but the oil could also be used when corpses were prepared for burial. Thus there was a suggestion of the cross.

Faith and discipleship

1 The first disciples were Andrew, Simon, James and John. Jesus told them to leave their nets and follow him.

2 They were to take a staff, no money or food, their sandals and only one shirt. The idea was that they should travel light, moving on from place to place.

3 Peter denied knowing Jesus three times. His failure gives Christians hope that they will be forgiven when they fail.

4 The Ascension suggested that Jesus had authority over creation and was the Messiah.

Significance and importance

1 The Kingdom of God is present now in the world, will come fully in the future and is also at work within people

2 The following people were reckoned as being outside the Kingdom: Gentiles, Tax Collectors, women with an issue of blood, lepers and Samaritans.

3 Jesus shocked people by touching and healing a leper.

4 Jesus showed his authority to forgive sins in the story of the paralysed man being let down through the roof. The Pharisees commented that Jesus taught with authority.

Notes

Notes

Commentaries on Exam Practice answers at www.hoddereducation.co.uk/myrevisionnotes